JAMAICA

JAMAICA

MANAGING POLITICAL AND ECONOMIC CHANGE

John D. Forbes

American Enterprise Institute for Public Policy Research
Washington and London

John D. Forbes is a career U.S. Foreign Service officer who has served in Vietnam, the Philippines, and Jamaica as well as the Department of State in Washington. From 1980 to 1983 he was political counselor at the American Embassy in Kingston. This study was prepared during the academic year 1983–1984, which the author spent as a fellow at the Center for International Affairs, Harvard University. The views expressed are his own and do not necessarily reflect official positions of the Department of State.

The publication of this monograph was aided by a grant from the Mellon Foundation to AEI's Center for Hemispheric Studies.

To Christian, who shared many enriching experiences with his father in Jamaica.

ISBN 0–8447–1100–4

Library of Congress Catalog Card No. 84–73179
Special Analysis No. 85–1

Printed in the United States of America

CONTENTS

PREFACE

Jamaica is a test case in the Caribbean, both for American foreign policy and for the possibilities of democratic development. The largest of the English-speaking Antillean islands, Jamaica has significant resources and potential; yet its democratic institutions, shaped in the Westminster tradition, were strongly strained in the 1970s, and the possibilities for renewed polarization and fragmentation have continued into the 1980s. Particularly in the aftermath of the U.S. Grenada action of 1983, the outcome of Jamaica's political struggle will be closely watched in the rest of the Caribbean. That President Reagan singled out Jamaica for special treatment early in his administration gives added importance to the Jamaican experiment.

In this monograph John D. Forbes traces the evolution of Jamaica's development with particular attention to the contemporary period. He assesses the colonial legacy, the origins of Jamaica's two-party system, and Jamaica's early years of self-rule; he examines the island's growing prosperity and its rising social tension during the first decade of independence; and he discusses the socialist experimentation of the Michael Manley period and the crisis it provoked. In the 1980 election Edward Seaga defeated Manley and ushered in a period of more conservative rule. Forbes analyzes Jamaica's struggle to recover and its prospects in a fair, reasoned, and judicious way; his conclusions and recommendations for U.S. policy are similarly balanced and careful.

This is a well-written, serious study of an important country; we are pleased to include it in our special analyses series and to recommend it to scholars, students, and policy makers with interest in the Caribbean Basin.

HOWARD J. WIARDA
Resident Scholar and Director
Center for Hemispheric Studies

INTRODUCTION

After forty years of democratic political experience and twenty-two years of independence, Jamaica, the Caribbean's second most populous democracy, faces the most serious challenge of its modern history. Less than two decades ago, the newly independent country was considered a model of economic and political development in the third world. Economic growth was strong, and a viable two-party system permitted peaceful political change around a centrist policy consensus. Between 1950 and 1972 Jamaica experienced average annual economic growth of 7 percent, one of the highest rates among developing countries.

During the past ten years, however, Jamaica has acquired a very different image. The country has endured a period of considerable economic and political crisis. Its economy declined for seven successive years until 1981 by a total of 26 percent. The earlier political consensus disappeared, and the strength of Jamaican democracy was severely tested. Talk of the gradual "Haitianization" of the island replaced predictions of economic takeoff. Since 1981 Jamaica has had a reprieve from the disastrous decline of the 1970s but has yet to regain the promise of its first years of independence.

Like many developing countries, Jamaica is confronted with deep and perhaps intractable social, economic, and political problems. Health services and education are deteriorating. High unemployment has been chronic for decades. The principal productive sectors of the economy—manufacturing, mining, and agriculture—are performing far below capacity. Polarization between the two major political parties has been severe for ten years; political violence has become commonplace. Income distribution and landownership are badly skewed. Emigration is high, and capital flight drains the economy. Many Jamaicans have little confidence in the future of their country.

Yet Jamaica is an island of considerable potential, with significant mineral, climatic, geographic, and human resources. It can achieve sustained economic growth and once again set an example of successful development if it can overcome the difficult obstacles that block its progress. To understand the challenge facing Jamaica today, some appreciation of its history as well as the background to its present situation is necessary. The key factors essential, in my view, to long-term economic prosperity and political stability conclude this study.

3

1

The Colonial Legacy

Jamaica's twenty-two years of independence are a brief period in contrast to the more than four and a half centuries of European colonial rule. Spain controlled Jamaica until the middle of the seventeenth century, but the Spanish did not emphasize the development of the island, and little remains of their influence. Instead, three centuries of British rule deeply molded and influenced present-day Jamaica. The island became Britain's most important possession in the West Indies, with a prosperous plantation economy based on sugar and slave labor. In the 1700s Jamaica was the world's largest producer of sugar.

The influence that slavery and the plantation economy have had and still have on Jamaica should not be underestimated. Most settlers in Britain's North American colonies migrated voluntarily, founding communities of small farmers, artisans, and traders with early democratic traditions. Jamaica and other European colonies in the Caribbean had totally different experiences. Their populations were built by forced migration and violence. Over 90 percent of Jamaica's 1982 population of 2.2 million is of African and African-European descent. The small remainder consists of Europeans, East Indians, Chinese, Lebanese, and their mixtures. The Africans arrived as slave labor, the Europeans as plantation operators; the East Indians and Chinese came as indentured workers to ease the labor shortage on sugar estates that followed emancipation in 1834; and the Lebanese (known as Syrians in Jamaica) came as small traders in the early 1900s. There is also a small but influential Jewish community whose ancestry in Jamaica dates from the sixteenth century.

Despite the abolition of slavery 150 years ago, its effects still permeate Jamaican society. Attitudes of resentment toward authority as well as dependency on government, a tendency to denigrate agricultural and manual labor, and subtle color and class distinctions that continue despite intermarriage and increased social mobility all reflect the country's slave inheritance. Jamaica does not have the same historical or cultural traditions as its nearby North or Latin American neighbors. It is a predominantly African society transplanted violently to the Caribbean, with an overlay of British political, economic, and social tradition.

5

The British legacy is also evident in the class system and in the attitudes of the island's business class. For much of the country's history, the small minority made up of the largely white plantocracy enjoyed privileges reflecting its monopoly of political and economic power. In more recent years a sizable middle class, which is perhaps even more protective of its position than the upper class, has developed. Attitudes and patterns of behavior that derive from such class distinctions are only slowly fading and are likely to persist until far greater economic and social progress has been made. Upward mobility is possible but limited. A combination of lingering class and racial prejudice and inadequate local economic opportunity continues to stimulate a steady exodus from the island of part of its surplus population, most recently to the United States and Canada.[1]

Export agriculture and the commercial sector dominated economic activity in Jamaica during the British colonial period. Jamaica and other British colonies in the Caribbean fell into an economic pattern often followed by European colonizers, of large plantations producing a single export crop, with a protected market for the metropole's manufactured goods. In the West Indies sugar predominated; in Malaysia it was tin and in Ceylon, tea. Only in the last thirty years has the Jamaican economy become more diversified. The sugar economy long enjoyed guaranteed metropolitan markets and high prices, and comfortable profits were available to the commission agents who imported and exported goods, predominantly between Britain and Jamaica. Competition, innovation, and risk taking were thus not characteristics of the business tradition on the island. A strong preference for oligopolistic arrangements and high, predictable profits is still an important element of the business mentality in Jamaica.

Slavery, the class system, and the plantation economy under British rule produced essentially negative problems for contemporary, independent Jamaica to overcome. In contrast, the British heritage in the areas of government, political rights, and civil administration has been much more positive, providing the new nation with a solid democratic foundation on which to build. For forty years Jamaica has practiced a modified version of the Westminster parliamentary political model and has enjoyed, except during one recent period, a degree of political stability unusual in the third world. Two major political parties—the People's National Party (PNP) and the Jamaica Labour Party (JLP)—have regularly alternated in power in the ten general elections held since the introduction of universal adult suffrage in 1944. Turnout at the polls has been consistently high for four decades.

The rule of law is generally respected in Jamaica, despite considerable violence bred by unemployment, a breakdown in traditional extended family support systems, narcotics trafficking, inadequate law enforcement, and police excesses. But there is an ideal legal structure, which the political leadership, the elites, and most of the population support and strive to

6

abide by. The judicial system is well developed, even though many laws are antiquated and many courts overcrowded. Jamaicans, even the poorer ones, are often litigious, and an abundance of lawyers, most trained in England, keep the system functioning.

There is a deep attachment to the Jamaican Constitution, reflecting the prevailing respect for law and legal institutions. A military coup is virtually unthinkable. The major political parties may differ over the means by which Jamaica should become a republic—that is, over the division of powers between a president and a prime minister—but neither disputes the essential political framework of direct, periodic elections and the parliamentary system spelled out in the Constitution.

Political freedoms are highly valued by Jamaica's individualistic population, in part because of British tutelage and to some extent in reaction against the experience of slavery. A country made up of descendants of slaves assigns great importance to respect for individual liberties. Any Jamaican is free to express opinions, meet with others, form a political party, publish a newspaper, worship as he or she chooses, change jobs, move within the country, or travel abroad. The numerous human rights that the Jamaican Constitution recognizes are honored in practice to a surprising degree.[2]

Democratic traditions in Jamaica have become so strong that any effort to abridge popular political rights would meet strong condemnation and resistance. Jamaica is very unlikely to move in an authoritarian direction, either to the right or the left, even in the event of more severe economic setbacks. Support for nondemocratic political arrangements does exist, but only among the small political parties of the far left. The influence of these parties has waned in recent years, and they would have great difficulty in imposing authoritarian practices in the unlikely event that they were in a position to attempt to do so. The vast majority of the population, from the elite to the very poor, would oppose any serious abridgment of political freedoms or movement away from fundamental democratic practices as established in the Constitution. This reality imposes restraints on the party in power and gives the opposition great leverage in protecting itself against any efforts to restrict its freedom to perform the role of critic and alternative government.

The political legacy of British colonialism has therefore been a system of respect for law, human rights, and democratic government. The British also left Jamaica with a well-trained civil service, which has unfortunately deteriorated in quality but not in numbers in the past decade. Without question, these political assets are the most positive and lasting contribution Britain made to Jamaica and, for that matter, to many of its other former colonies, which today constitute a surprisingly large number of that minority of developing states that are nonauthoritarian. That Jamaica pos-

7

sesses a strong consensus on the transfer of political power through periodic elections significantly enhances both its political stability and its potential for economic development and stands in sharp contrast to such other states in the region as Haiti, Nicaragua, and—until recently—El Salvador.

2

ORIGINS OF THE TWO-PARTY SYSTEM AND
EARLY YEARS OF SELF-RULE

An understanding of contemporary Jamaican politics must start with the expansion of suffrage, the development of popular political organizations, and the unique role of two men in the preindependence period beginning more than forty years ago. Before the general elections of 1944, suffrage was based on ownership of land and on class and was largely restricted to the island's elite. In the seven general elections for the Legislative Assembly held between 1901 and 1935, a maximum of 7 percent of the population was registered to vote, and no more than 3 percent voted in any one election.[3] This small electorate sought to protect its interests as well as those of the British Crown, while the vast majority of the population had no direct political influence.

By the early 1930s popular discontent with harsh economic and social conditions on the island was growing, as was discussion of political and other reforms among those Jamaicans who would subsequently emerge as the new nationalist leaders. Neither mass political parties nor popular elections into which this discontent could be channeled existed at the time. Instead, the trade union became the first popular political organization in Jamaica. Between 1935 and 1938 extensive labor strife, especially among sugar and dock workers, dramatized conditions on the island and gave the poor a means of voicing dissatisfaction. In effect, this was the closest that Jamaica came to a "revolutionary" struggle against its colonial master, although there were only a few deaths. The country's nationalist movement originated in these years, as did the major trade unions and political parties of today. These labor disturbances of the late 1930s prompted London to send a royal commission to study conditions in Jamaica (and elsewhere in the West Indies). The commission's findings led in the early 1940s to better wages and to universal adult suffrage under a new constitution giving the island greater self-government.

The political history of Jamaica in the 1930s also saw the emergence of two powerful figures who were to dominate the country's politics for the next thirty years. Not until the late 1960s would a new generation of

9

leaders succeed the two founding fathers of independent Jamaica—William Alexander Bustamante and Norman Washington Manley. Though distant cousins, the two men had very different backgrounds and personalities.

Bustamante was a blustery, self-made populist, without a high-school diploma, who became prominent as a Kingston moneylender and the author of letters on populist themes in the country's leading newspaper. The trade union movement was his path to political power. In May 1938 he formed the Bustamante Industrial Trade Union (BITU), which he headed until his death three decades later. Autocratic and ambitious, Bustamante was the principal leader of the strikes for improved economic conditions and was eventually jailed by the British for his opposition. His BITU was the first organization to mobilize the island's working class.

In contrast, Norman Manley was a British-educated lawyer and Rhodes scholar. Athletic, articulate, and intellectual, he was far more reserved than Bustamante. Manley became the center of a group of middle-class reformers who sought greater political influence in the affairs of the colony. In September 1938 they founded Jamaica's first political party, the People's National Party (PNP).

Jamaica's two-party system has its roots in the political rivalry between these two men. Initially they worked together. Bustamante was a founding member of the PNP, and Manley supported the BITU. It is interesting to speculate that, had there been only one preeminent nationalist leader or had Manley and Bustamante continued their cooperation, Jamaica would most likely have become a one-party state with a different political history. The two broke with each other in February 1942, however, after the release from prison of Bustamante. He soon formed the Jamaica Labour Party (JLP), which successfully contested the first general election under universal adult suffrage. The new party drew primarily on the BITU for its organizational strength, an asset of considerable value since the BITU's membership in 1944 comprised 81 percent of the unionized work force.[4]

After its defeat in the 1944 elections, the PNP in 1945 formed its own mass labor organization, the Trade Union Congress (TUC), to rival the BITU. The TUC, however, was soon dominated by the PNP left wing and, after Manley forced the expulsion from the party of four prominent leftists in 1952, he organized the National Workers Union (NWU), which is today the principal rival of the larger BITU.

The split between Bustamante and Manley in 1942 was a watershed in Jamaican politics. From it came the entrenched two-party system and two dominant, competitive trade unions. Extreme political polarization between the two parties, however, is a more recent development, which the two early leaders avoided. The two-party system is indirectly acknowledged in Jamaica's 1962 Constitution, which, while making no mention of political parties per se, establishes the position of leader of the opposition in the

House of Representatives and gives its holder the right to name eight of the twenty-one members of the Senate. Most observers believe that each of the two parties enjoys the support of roughly 40 percent of the electorate, the remaining 20 percent constituting a bloc of swing voters who determine which party wins national elections. The degree of entrenchment of the two parties is such that they have alternated in power after two terms in office since 1944. Third parties and independents have had a history largely of electoral failure. During the forty years since 1944, the JLP has been in power twenty-four years and the PNP sixteen.[5]

Until the mid-1970s the two parties were more similar than different in policy, organization, and appeal. Both depended on organized trade unions for much of their electoral machinery and were therefore highly responsive to the interests of organized labor. Both were heavily financed by certain of the island's wealthiest families, who traditionally support one or the other party. The Ashenheim, Facey, Henriques, and Marzouca families, for example, have usually supported the JLP, while the Desnoe, Hanna, Issa, and Matalon families have frequently contributed to the PNP. Virtually all these families are from minority groups. Both parties followed similar centrist, moderately reformist, and pro-Western policies when in office, although the PNP has since its inception been a declared socialist party while the JLP has avoided developing a distinct ideology and prides itself on its pragmatism. After the PNP found in the 1944 campaign that its more radical positions had little popular appeal, it shifted toward the center in 1949 and remained there until moving to the left in 1974.

During the twenty-five years between 1949 and 1974, Jamaican politics were dominated by two similar, broadly based political parties with roughly equal popular followings, each enjoying the financial backing of large business interests and having a major trade union affiliate. The two parties, like two teams of administrators, regularly alternated in power but did not offer the Jamaican electorate any dramatic choice of social and economic policy. For almost thirty years most Jamaicans seemed satisfied with this arrangement.

Jamaica's first election under universal adult suffrage in 1944 saw a surprisingly heavy turnout of newly enfranchised voters. Thirty-one percent of the population participated, a percentage fifteen times as great as in the last election under restricted suffrage. Bustamante's JLP swept the polls, winning twenty-two seats to five for the PNP and five for independents. By 1949 the PNP had dropped the unpopular radical positions it had advocated in 1944 and had begun to organize a trade union affiliate in hopes of matching the influence among the electorate that the BITU gave to the JLP. In the 1949 elections the PNP made strong gains, winning thirteen seats, but Bustamante stayed in office as the JLP held seventeen seats.

11

The 1955 elections brought the PNP to office for the first time, by a margin of eighteen to fourteen seats, and initiated the pattern of alternation between the parties every two terms. Manley headed the government for seven years, winning reelection in 1959. In early 1962, two years before the end of his second term, he lost elections that he called because of the defeat in 1961 of a national referendum seeking approval of continued Jamaican membership in the West Indies Federation. The JLP won twenty-six of the forty-five constituencies. Jamaica became independent on August 5, 1962, and the JLP leader Bustamante became its first prime minister.

The preindependence period of increasing self-rule from 1944 to 1962 was quiet politically. The difficulties of the war years and the introduction of universal adult suffrage defused the growing popular political pressures that had surfaced in the labor disputes of the 1930s. Political participation by virtue of the broadened franchise and the growing strength of trade unions and political parties gave the masses at least a feeling of greater influence over domestic affairs. Yet little fundamental change in the society and no major attempts at economic and social reform occurred during this period. There were moderate improvements in public health and education, and the decade before independence was one of steady economic growth. The economy diversified substantially as new mining and manufacturing sectors, led by the development of bauxite and import substitution, as well as tourism, reduced the relative importance of traditional agriculture (principally sugar, bananas, and copra), which had long been the country's main economic activity. From 1950 to 1966 Jamaica received foreign investments of US$406.6 million, 58 percent of which went into the mining sector.

As London granted Jamaica increasing self-rule, reaching full internal self-government in 1957, the Bustamante and Manley administrations followed conservative policies, overseeing modest public programs financed within available resources and seeking to attract foreign investment, all under the general and benign tutelage of London. The excited political activity of the 1930s seemed to have achieved some important political if not many economic goals, and the preindependence decades of the 1940s and 1950s were comparatively strife free.

3

THE FIRST DECADE OF INDEPENDENCE:
PROSPERITY AND RISING TENSION

Full political independence in 1962 brought the new nation responsibility for its affairs but little other change in its situation. The transition was peaceful. When the black, green, and gold Jamaican flag replaced the Union Jack under the eyes of Princess Margaret (and American Vice President Lyndon Johnson), relatively little was different. There had been no violent independence struggle to wrest power from the British, nor were foreigners and their property driven away. In the absence of any national catharsis, there were no wounds to heal and no economy to rebuild. The politics of the new nation remained under the control of two leading personalities and their Eurocentric political parties, which had chosen a slightly modified Westminster parliamentary system as the political model upon which to build the country's Constitution. Today Jamaica remains a monarchy, with the queen of Jamaica, Elizabeth II, as head of state.

The JLP government in power at the time of independence carried on the policies of the preceding period. The economic growth of the 1950s continued. By 1965 manufacturing had grown from its infancy twenty years before to contribute 15 percent of the gross domestic product.[6] The bauxite-alumina industry, nonexistent in 1950, contributed 10 percent to GDP in 1965. Tourism completed this triad of economic diversification, as the number of visitors to the island more than quadrupled between 1950 and 1965.

Emigration, primarily to England, was substantial in the decade before independence, totaling 164,000 between 1950 and 1961, draining off excess labor and pushing down the unemployment rate from 25 percent in 1943 to 13.5 percent in 1960. Most of the economic growth during this period was stimulated by heavy foreign investment, principally from the United States and Canada. But the jobs created by new investment were not enough to match the growth in the island's labor force of some 20,000 annually. When emigration to the United Kingdom was virtually cut off in the middle of the decade, unemployment began to rise again, reaching 23.5 percent by 1972, the year the People's National Party returned to power. Moreover, the 50 percent of the island's population engaged in agriculture received few of the benefits from growth in other sectors of the economy. Public sector spending grew during the 1960s as the newly independent government began to borrow and tax more to provide increased services to the population.

Thus the decade of rule by the Jamaica Labour Party from 1962 to 1972 was one of growing prosperity for the upper and expanding middle classes and for those workers who filled new jobs created by investment. The poorer majority of the population benefited much less but nevertheless saw an improvement in its living standards. Popular material expectations were being pushed upward, however, by the example of the more prosperous elements in the society. The trickle-down effect has never worked very well in Jamaica. Instead, the middle class expands during prosperous times and competes for scarce foreign exchange to satisfy its appetite for imported consumer goods, often at the expense of imports for productive purposes. Despite the steady economic growth of the 1960s, social discontent grew, manifesting itself in crime and vicious political gang warfare in Kingston in 1966, which led to a two-month state of emergency. In 1968 riots in Kingston caused property damage amounting to several million dollars. Political comment began to focus on how to correct the glaring inequities in the society.

The JLP administration was reelected in 1967 by a narrow popular vote margin of 51 percent to 49 percent, increasing its majority in Parliament to thirty-three seats to twenty for the PNP. The JLP saw a change in leadership in the mid-1960s. Bustamante, whose health was failing, named Finance Minister Donald Sangster acting prime minister in 1966, but Sangster died less than two months after being sworn in as prime minister after the JLP electoral victory in 1967. The man who would serve as prime minister for the next five years was a Bustamante protégé, Hugh Shearer, a career trade unionist and politician who became president of the BITU after Bustamante's death.[7] Under Shearer economic growth continued, but his administration gained a reputation for weak management, factionalism, and corruption, thereby weakening the cause of the JLP in the 1972 elections. During these two JLP terms in office, Edward Seaga, a Harvard-educated Syrian-Jamaican with an early interest in sociology who turned to national politics in his mid-twenties, became nationally prominent, first as minister of development and welfare and later as minister of finance. Seaga, at age forty-four, replaced Shearer as leader of the JLP in 1974.

In the late 1960s both political parties underwent leadership transitions after almost three decades under the tutelage of Bustamante and Manley. The contribution of these two men—dissimilar in background and personality but remarkably alike in political outlook—to modern Jamaica warrants the recognition they have received as national heroes. Through strong leadership and similar policies, they gave their country remarkable political stability and sustained economic growth at a time when Jamaicans were beginning their experience of self-rule and independence. Both men were realistic nationalists with a keen feeling for the difficult and modest role of their new nation in the world. They sought and largely achieved gradual improvement in living standards for the island's population without sudden, destabilizing change, and they managed to run the government in a way that gave both citizens and outsiders confidence in the future of the new Caribbean nation. In the less than two decades since Bustamante and Manley stepped aside, Jamaica has passed through very different times, suffering extensive economic decline and reaching a nadir of near civil war in the violence of the 1980 election campaign.

The PNP chose in 1969 to stay with the Manley name and elected Norman Manley's son Michael to succeed his late father as party president. Educated at the London School of Economics, he was deeply influenced by Harold Laski and socialist political and economic prescriptions for the emerging colonial areas. Young Manley had a brief career in journalism, with the BBC and in Jamaica with the PNP's newspaper, before concentrating on trade union work. He assisted his father in forming the National Workers Union, in which he held the key position of island supervisor from 1955 to 1972. Manley has a quick mind, strong charisma, and a gift for oratory, which have proved to be highly useful political assets. The new leader of the JLP was Shearer, like Manley a trade union leader who had built a political career on strong negotiating skills and extensive organizational influence derived from his union base.[8]

4

The Michael Manley Period: Socialist Experimentation and Crisis

By 1972 and the end of a decade of Jamaica Labour Party government, Jamaica seemed ready to repeat the pattern of alternating between the People's National Party and the JLP every two elections. Shearer and his party waited until the constitutional maximum period between elections of five years before holding general elections in 1972. The JLP campaigned on the basis of the strong economic growth in the 1960s and the expansion of education and other government services during its two terms in office.

But positive economic growth was insufficient to win the JLP an unprecedented third term in office. Rising unemployment and the growing appeal of populist politics hurt the government among a large proportion of the lower classes, while corruption and a tarnished reputation for management weakened its support among the middle and upper classes. The business elite, alienated by JLP taxation and nationalization policies, which it viewed as threatening to its interests, generously financed the PNP campaign. In addition, bitter factional infighting in the JLP prevented the party from uniting solidly behind Shearer.

The prosperity of the 1960s worked against the incumbent government because the benefits of economic growth were not distributed widely among the electorate. As rural isolation was eroded and rural-urban migration accelerated, the material expectations of voters increased. Thus the majority who did not see themselves as better off in relation to the prospering upper and middle classes responded enthusiastically to Manley's slogan "Better Must Come."

Eager for a change in leadership, the country swung sharply to the opposition PNP, which captured thirty-seven of the fifty-three seats in the House of Representatives and 56 percent of the popular vote. The margin would have been higher, in view of the PNP's strong appeal to the country's youth, had the voters' list not been four years out of date, thereby restricting the electorate to registered voters twenty-five years of age and older. During the campaign opposition leader Manley skillfully developed populist themes (such as "power to the people" and "the word is love"),

16

which appealed widely to Jamaican voters and convinced many that his leadership could achieve both greater social justice and continued economic prosperity.

Manley was attractive, and so were his ideas. His appeal to the unsophisticated poor was obvious, and many in the middle and business classes also swung behind him because of disenchantment with the JLP government, fascination with his charisma, and a belief that Manley would make Jamaica a better country. To many of the ghetto dwellers and small farmers he was a messiah, holding out the promise of an end to their suffering. Indeed, he adopted the biblical name Joshua to persuade the fundamentalist Christian population of his messianic potential to transform society and lead the country out of its wilderness to a new promised land. His hold on the country was so great in 1972 and 1973 that one commentator wrote that much of the population would willingly have followed the new prime minister had he marched into the Caribbean Sea.

Coming to power at the beginning of his country's second decade of independence, Manley was the first leader to make Jamaicans feel that they could control their country's destiny and significantly restructure the economic and social system they had inherited from colonial rule. Despite nearly thirty years of self-rule and considerable economic growth, most Jamaicans in 1972 were dissatisfied with their society and welcomed reformist proposals. Manley's campaign promises and skillful public relations once in office led to high popular expectations of improvement. His subsequent failure to live up to what the country had been led to believe he could accomplish made the disillusionment of many of his supporters all the greater.

Manley eventually proved to be a messiah who lost his way to the promised land, in the eyes of some, or a Judas who had betrayed their hopes and trust, in the view of many others. Dissatisfaction with his leadership and policies among some influential supporters began as early as 1974 and steadily increased thereafter, particularly as the PNP turned to the left. In the end, in 1980, the country was attracted to new leadership, again placing exaggerated hopes in the ability of a political leader to produce better times.

The messiah syndrome is still very characteristic of Jamaican democracy. During election campaigns the principal party leaders promise significant improvements if elected, and the winner eventually faces disillusioned and impatient voters whose heightened expectations of the government have been unfulfilled. Pandering to popular wishes is a habit of politicians in many countries, but unlike most third world states, Jamaica does have regular elections as well as a strong tradition of democratic opposition. Together these exert pressure on the governing party to be sensitive to public opinion if it wishes to retain power and to work hard to achieve the usually unrealistic promises it has made to the electorate.

During Manley's two terms in office, from 1972 to 1980, the PNP government attempted ambitious reforms to improve social conditions and to restructure the economy. Manley sought in effect to change Jamaica in a few years into a highly socialized, egalitarian state but lacked the necessary financial and management resources for the task.

Despite the economic deterioration Jamaica suffered in the 1970s, Manley and his defenders have few regrets today about the correctness of their policies. They blame real and imaginary external factors (such as "destabilization") for much of their failure and say they intend to follow the same policy agenda, though with an improved sense of priorities, when they return to power. Critics on the far left believe Manley's policies failed because they were not sufficiently radical in addressing the social, economic, and political problems of the country. In the end, however, the PNP lost in 1980 not because the country rejected socialism per se but because it disapproved of the poor performance of the Manley government, especially in the economic area. Had Manley been successful in accomplishing his ambitious domestic programs, he might still be prime minister.

DOMESTIC POLICY AND THE ECONOMY

The initiatives of the Manley administration touched most sectors of society and won the new prime minister considerable popularity for a period. The public sector grew steadily, both in expenditure and in direct employment, as an increasing number of publicly financed programs were created. In agriculture an attempt at land redistribution was intended to convert idle land to productive use by small farmers and to establish workers' cooperatives on sugar estates owned by the government. The state became owner of all public utilities and public transportation and a range of businesses from hotels to a dairy to an airline catering service. State ownership of public utilities and agricultural lands had begun under the JLP regime but was greatly accelerated under the PNP government, which believed in a strong public sector that controlled the "commanding heights" of the economy and was usually willing to purchase a failing business to maintain employment. While there were no instances of uncompensated expropriation of private property, owners often contended that they received far less than market value. Many unemployed Jamaicans were put on the government payroll as casual workers, in line with the populist view that every citizen had a right to a job.

A major campaign was waged against adult illiteracy, and free secondary education was introduced as the government increased its control of private schools. Workers received more generous bargaining rights and a minimum wage law, and a two-month paid maternity leave was introduced. A controversial property tax was levied but poorly enforced. Many of these programs were fundamentally flawed; others became controversial not so much for their purpose but because of the poor manner in which they were carried out and the waste and expense to the taxpayer. Too much was attempted in too short a time with too few resources.

Agriculture is an example of how the PNP's well-intentioned programs, when improperly administered, had wasteful and unintended results. Much of the idle land purchased by the PNP government and its predecessor remained idle, as it does today. In a much-publicized program, Pioneer Farms were established to give jobless youth opportunities to farm. These youngsters usually occupied their new land but did not receive appropriate training and assistance to become successful small crop farmers; some recipients were chosen by political criteria and had little real interest in farming.

The division of some banana plantations into smaller plots gave individual farmers land, but their inability to meet rigorous export standards meant that their produce flooded the local market and less foreign exchange was earned. The twenty-three new sugar cooperatives operated in the red, as did the state-owned sugar estates and factories, which suffered from antiquated equipment, poor management, and excess labor. From 1972 to 1980 sugar production dropped from 4 million to 2.7 million tons; banana production plummeted from 370,000 tons in 1972 to 172,000 tons in 1979 and 69,000 tons in 1980, when a severe hurricane swept through the major areas of production. Many years of neglect have hurt these two traditional export crops; but poor public management, the shift to cooperatives, and land redistribution under the Manley government caused production to fall, both absolutely and per acre, and reduced foreign exchange earnings.

The poor performance of the PNP administration stood in sharp contrast to the ambitious goals of reform and transformation it had set for the country. Elected because of populist demands for reform, to which he responded, Manley was eventually defeated by the severe deterioration of the economy. Jamaica did not increase its export production sufficiently to pay for needed imports, which were rising rapidly in price. The result was a decline in imports as foreign exchange became scarcer, eventually crippling the economy and leading to greatly increased borrowing. Domestically, the government ran continuing inflationary deficits. Living standards fell. Real per capita GDP declined every year from 1974 through 1980, falling by a total of 26 percent for the seven-year period. Net international reserves, which had been positive in 1972, dropped to minus US$857 million by 1980. External debt rose from US$349 million in 1973 to US$1.3 billion in 1980, or 49 percent of GDP.

The bauxite-alumina sector, which had been a key stimulus to growth in the 1950s and 1960s, stopped expanding in the 1970s after Jamaica imposed a levy that made Jamaican bauxite less competitive internationally and resulted in producers' increasing their operations in other countries. Jamaica's share of worldwide bauxite and alumina production fell significantly by the end of the decade, when bauxite production had dropped 21 percent from its 1974 peak performance. Nevertheless, Manley's bauxite policy was successful in the short run. Coming in the wake of the oil price shock, it increased several-fold the revenue to Jamaica from its mining sector, and the Jamaican government gained an ownership stake in the country's principal natural resource by acquiring bauxite lands from the companies. Unfortunately, this new income, though intended to stimulate the growth of industry through a Capital Development Fund, was to a great extent channeled into politically popular public spending programs.

In a related initiative, Manley took the lead in establishing the International Bauxite Association, headquartered in Kingston, which he hoped could follow in the footsteps of OPEC. Although most major bauxite-producing countries joined, the IBA has not functioned successfully as a cartel for a variety of reasons, not the least of which is that bauxite is an extremely common mineral, the demand for which was about to fall because of the world recession at the time the IBA was being organized.

Public spending, largely for new social programs, increased fivefold by 1980, even though roads, public utilities, schools, hospitals, and other public buildings were inadequately maintained. Manufacturing in 1980 was one-third below the peak year of 1973. Inflation averaged 22 percent per year during the period. Capital conservatively estimated at US$500 million left the island, and tens of thousands of skilled Jamaicans migrated, some moving their families to Miami and commuting each week to their businesses in Kingston. Crime and violence increased sharply, leading to the draconian but largely ineffective Gun Court legislation, which required mandatory life imprisonment for illegal possession of firearms or ammunition.

While traditional economic activity foundered, the export of marijuana to North America was allowed to flourish after a brief but successful U.S.-Jamaican eradication campaign in 1976. By the end of the decade this illegal activity was widespread throughout the island and indirectly supported a surprising amount of the economic activity requiring imported materials, at a time when foreign exchange was otherwise extremely scarce.

The unemployment rate did not increase by as much as might have been expected during the Manley administration, largely because public sector employment and spending grew and migration to North America continued. In 1972 unemployment stood at 23.2 percent and in 1980 at 27.4 percent. If one takes the 13 percent increase in population during the same period into account, however, this rate meant that the total number of unemployed workers had risen by more than 100,000.

Government waste and inappropriate policies were not the only reasons for the economic decline of the 1970s. External economic factors had a serious negative effect on the Jamaican economy and came as a severe blow, at an early stage, to the Manley government. Jamaica depends on imported oil for 99 percent of its commercial energy, and the rise in oil prices that began in 1973 caused havoc. The country's oil bill tripled in two years and by 1980 was almost nine times what it had been in 1972. The subsequent recession in industrial countries and rising interest rates for external borrowing created further difficulties, while the prices of Jamaica's exports did not rise commensurately with the cost of imports. Other democracies in the Caribbean, such as the Bahamas, Barbados, and the Dominican Republic, however, managed to achieve economic growth in this period.

The oil price rise posed an early and unexpected challenge to the Manley government, threatening to cripple its reform program before it began. But instead of exercising fiscal and monetary restraint in the face of a worsening balance of payments, the government pressed ahead with costly social programs. Then in 1974 the PNP adopted a more ideological approach, which was eventually to destroy the confidence of important elements of Jamaican society in the Manley administration. In November 1974 the PNP launched what it described as a new ideology for the party under the rubric Democratic Socialism, spelling out thirteen principles the party intended to pursue and explain to the country in an unprecedented political education campaign. The new ideology constituted a sharp turn to the left, departing from the greater pragmatism of the PNP under Norman Manley and immediately giving the party and the government a more radical socialist image. The changes came at a time when black power and radical nationalism were becoming more influential in the English-speaking Caribbean, and the shift to the left was in part an attempt to co-opt such trends within the PNP.

No doubt the new political philosophy of the PNP, combined with Manley's continuing charismatic appeal, contributed greatly to his popularity in the third world, where he soon emerged as a champion of the new international economic order (NIEO). But at home the emphasis on class and ideological struggle alarmed many upper- and middle-class Jamaicans, already disturbed by worsening economic conditions, and began to stimulate an exodus of capital and skills that was to bleed the country. Manley's irritable response to those who disagreed with his policies was summed up when he reminded his critics that "there are five flights a day to Miami." Manley soon acquired the image of an anti-American, anticapitalist champion of third world socialism. Perhaps this aided his leadership aspirations in the Non-Aligned movement, the Socialist International, and similar groups, but it hurt his chances of political and economic success at home.

Just as Manley viewed his domestic policy as a third path in the Caribbean between the examples of Puerto Rican capitalist development and Cuban state authoritarianism, he believed Jamaica should pursue a foreign policy neutral between East and West and end what the PNP after 1974 described as a foreign policy reflecting "a servile relationship with imperialism."[9] Manley's activism in foreign policy was not surprising, nor was his interest in drawing attention to the problems of third world countries, and he became a leading spokesman for the NIEO and other positions favored by the Non-Aligned movement. In shifting away from Jamaica's traditional pro-Western foreign policy, however, Manley often moved to the extreme positions of more radical states such as Cuba, thereby bringing Jamaican foreign policy into disagreement on many issues with the West and especially the United States. Within the immediate Caribbean region, Jamaica by the end of the decade supported the New Jewel movement in Grenada, the Sandinistas in Nicaragua, and antigovernment rebels in El Salvador. The tilt in Manley's foreign policy to the left, toward Havana and away from Washington, was pronounced.

The most controversial PNP foreign policy initiative concerned relations with Jamaica's nearest neighbor, Cuba. Consular relations with Cuba had been opened a few years after independence by the JLP government. In 1972 Jamaica, along with Barbados, Guyana, and Trinidad and Tobago, agreed to exchange ambassadors with Cuba. Manley and Cuban President Fidel Castro soon developed a friendship, beginning when Manley traveled to the 1973 Algiers Non-Aligned summit on Castro's airplane. Manley visited Cuba in 1975, Castro made a state visit to Jamaica in 1977, and the two still meet from time to time. The far left within the PNP, led by former General Secretary D. K. Duncan, developed very close ties to the Cuban Communist party. They admired Cuba's successful social programs and political mobilization while ignoring its restrictions on political rights and its economic failures. A self-styled black-power, Marxist revolutionary, Duncan was openly sympathetic to Cuba and frequently urged his party colleagues to follow Cuban examples. Duncan headed the short-lived Ministry of National Mobilization, which was intended to stimulate broad support for the government's social programs among the civil service and other groups.

In the mid-1970s Cuba sought to expand its role in Jamaica. It dispatched to Kingston an activist ambassador, Ulises Estrada, with a past history of intelligence and special military assignments. Three dozen medical personnel were sent to rural Jamaican hospitals, and 400 construction workers arrived to build three high schools. Some 1,200 young Jamaicans were sent to Cuba for construction training as part of the Brigadista program; most returned home to discover they could not find employment for their new skills in the deteriorating Jamaican economy. Several hundred high-school graduates from poor families were awarded college scholarships to study in Cuba. These Cuban aid programs were essentially political in purpose. Cuba, after all, was no more developed than Jamaica but had an essentially negative reputation among the Jamaican population, which the aid and extensive publicity given to each project in government-controlled media sought to change.[10]

Cuba also conducted clandestine activities in Jamaica, which were not publicized at the time and have never been officially acknowledged by either Cuba or the PNP. Several hundred Brigadistas, handpicked for their political reliability, received special military training in Cuba. In 1980 and 1981 Jamaican security forces captured hundreds of M-16 rifles whose serial numbers matched records of weapons sent to Vietnam and presumably captured by the present Vietnamese government in 1975. There is strong reason to believe that these weapons were sent to Cuba and eventually smuggled into Jamaica with the complicity of the far left of the PNP for use by gunmen working with the PNP during the violent 1980 election campaign. These high-powered weapons introduced a new level of violence into Jamaican politics.

Ambassador Estrada became a highly controversial local figure. He was often seen in the close company of Manley, Manley's wife Beverly (a political radical who headed the party's women's movement), and PNP General Secretary Duncan. Estrada's behavior and statements were openly pro-PNP, and he soon became a target both for opponents of the PNP and for some PNP moderates who were suspicious of Cuba's increasing influence in Jamaica.[11] Jamaica's leading independent newspaper, the *Daily Gleaner*, frequently criticized the ties between the Manley government and Cuba and singled out Estrada. In an unusual response, Manley led his cabinet in 1979 in a march on the *Gleaner*'s offices in downtown Kingston to protest the paper's attacks on the Cuban diplomat. By 1980 "fear of Communism" had become a major political issue, fanned by the opposition JLP, which was to hurt the PNP badly at the polls.

If Jamaica's relations with Cuba improved considerably during the period of PNP government, those with the United States deteriorated badly. This was particularly unfortunate since, even before independence, the United States had become the country with which Jamaica's external relations were most extensive. The United States was Jamaica's largest trading partner, its principal source of foreign investment and tourists, home to a large community of Jamaican immigrants, and the favored destination of

Jamaican travelers and students. U.S. banks were major lenders to the Jamaican government, and the United States had provided economic assistance to Jamaica for many years, a total of US$120 million from 1956 to 1980. The United States is by far the most admired country among Jamaicans. Maintaining good relations with such an influential neighbor should therefore be of major political and economic importance to the government in power in Kingston. From the U.S. perspective, Jamaica was of interest for several reasons. It was the most significant of the newly independent, democratic, English-speaking Caribbean states, was located close to vital shipping lanes, supplied more than half the bauxite imported into the United States, and had more than US$1 billion in U.S. investment, mostly in the bauxite-alumina and tourist industries.

The sources of Manley's opposition to the U.S. government are unclear, but it seems to derive from his "progressive" analysis of Jamaica's economic and social conditions, his strong criticism of U.S. foreign policy, and his ambition to speak for third world radicalism. Given his socialist political philosophy, he mistrusted the leading capitalist power. Manley came to see himself as something of a Caribbean David versus the Goliath of the United States; he emphasized what he saw as the negative aspects of the relationship instead of seeking means of cooperation. His view of U.S. policy in the Caribbean is exemplified by his 1982 book *Jamaica: Struggle in the Periphery,* the cover of which features an eagle swooping southward from the American mainland with talons enveloping Jamaica.[12] He saw Jamaica as "on the receiving end of the imperialist whip" and his loss of power in the 1980 elections as delivering "the country once again fully into the hands of imperialist interests."[13]

Various American entities became convenient scapegoats for Manley and the PNP left as the situation at home deteriorated. "Destabilization," first by the United States and later by the JLP opposition, became a favorite Manley catchword. The aluminum companies were accused of destabilizing Jamaica when they located new operations in other countries after the bauxite levy was imposed. The U.S. press was charged with destabilizing tourism and investment when it published unfavorable articles about Jamaica. And, of course, the U.S. government and the CIA were Manley's favorite bêtes noires, whom he saw as masterminding a campaign intended to unseat him and his progressive government. None but the most circumstantial or contrived evidence was cited to support the destabilization argument, but that seemed to matter little.[14] Innuendo and constant comparisons between Jamaica and Chile and Manley and Salvador Allende, inspired by the PNP and others of the far left, damaged bilateral relations while falling on increasingly unreceptive domestic ears.

Leftist ideological influence had taken hold within high levels of the PNP after 1974 to an unprecedented extent. All too often the party expended energies debating ideological fine points instead of practical realities. The proper definition of U.S. imperialism and the reasons that the Soviet Union was a more benign superpower than the United States became two popular issues for party discussion. Where his father had fought hard and successfully to expel the far left from the PNP in 1952, Michael Manley behaved in the opposite fashion, promoting the Marxist Duncan to the key position of general secretary and putting a Cuban-trained activist in charge of the party's youth organization. It seems unlikely that Manley himself had deep Communist sympathies; but there is no doubt that some of his entourage had such sympathies and also close links with the small, pro-Moscow Communist Workers' Party of Jamaica (WPJ), headed by Oxford-educated Trevor Monroe, a professor at the University of the West Indies.

The combination of a declining economy and leftist rhetoric caused the flow of new foreign investment in Jamaica to cease, falling from US$175 million in 1971 to negative amounts from 1975 onward, and stimulated the flight of capital and skilled personnel from the country. Rhetoric, though often not backed by action, nevertheless created an impression of hostility to foreign investors and tourists. Rather than address these problems in any fundamental way, Manley saw in them evidence of the destabilization theory he propounded and for the most part continued the rhetoric and policies that had contributed to the country's growing crisis. Manley summarized his view of the circumstances he faced as follows: "Clearly, the multinational corporation, the conservative elements of the Western press, the champions of the capitalist system, the US establishment and those who defended the status quo generally, were lined up solidly behind the JLP."[15]

THE 1976 ELECTIONS AND THEIR AFTERMATH

Despite the lengthening economic shadows over the country, the PNP was able to win a second term in the 1976 elections, capturing forty-seven of the sixty seats in the House of Representatives and 57 percent of the popular vote. The elections were preceded by more political violence than Jamaica had previously experienced, for which both parties shared responsibility. Polarization and bitterness between the two parties increased substantially as the PNP moved to the left and after Seaga became JLP leader in 1974.

Several unusual political steps favored the PNP in these elections. First, the voting age was lowered in 1974 from twenty-one to eighteen, thereby enfranchising politically impressionable youth inclined to be swayed by the populism of the PNP. Jamaica's leading political pollster, Carl Stone, found in a preelection poll that 1972 voters favored the JLP;

but the PNP had such a large lead among youth that he predicted it would win easily.

Second, six months before the election Manley declared a state of emergency, charging that the JLP was plotting a campaign of violence and arresting or deporting several JLP candidates and numerous party activists. The evidence against the JLP was weak, but the government's action hampered the legitimate political activities of the opposition and tarnished its reputation in the eyes of a public concerned by growing political violence.

Third, shortly before the election, constituency boundaries were redrawn in an act of gerrymandering that shifted pro-JLP voting districts in several marginal PNP seats into adjacent pro-JLP constituencies. Then, on election day, there was extensive ballot-box stuffing in some constituencies; the opposition eventually legally challenged the results in thirteen of the forty-seven races it lost.[16]

Although these measures improved the PNP's chances of winning, they were probably unnecessary, except for lowering the voting age. Despite rising disenchantment with his government since 1974, Manley was still popular with much of the electorate, both for his personal appeal and for his many new social programs, which by that time had either been introduced or been promised with considerable fanfare.

The election of 1976 was the first in which the JLP campaigned under its new leader, Edward Seaga, who did not have the charisma nor the rhetorical skills of Manley. From his record as a minister in the JLP government of the 1960s and from his vocal role in opposition, Seaga had built a reputation as a pragmatic technocrat and financial expert. But in 1976 a majority of the electorate were still attached to the PNP and believed that its policies would help the country's poor in particular.

In 1977 the economic situation in Jamaica worsened, and the PNP government turned reluctantly to the International Monetary Fund (IMF) for help, negotiating a two-year standby loan of US$74 million. As conditions for the loan, the Jamaican dollar was devalued, and public spending increases were curtailed. In a political move designed to defend the ruling party against charges that it was moving too far to the left, the controversial Duncan was replaced as general secretary, but he remained active behind the scenes until restored to his position in 1979.

Relations with Washington and the new Carter administration improved considerably, and a three-year-old hold on additional U.S. assistance to Jamaica ended. Manley was attracted by the new emphasis in Washington on human rights and the problems of the third world; he was especially pleased that his friend Andrew Young was appointed U.S. permanent representative to the United Nations. Washington during this period became more concerned with economic problems in the Caribbean and decided to assist the beleaguered Manley government. A quick $10 million aid request was sent to the Congress, and in FY 1978 and FY 1979 requests for Jamaica reached $63.3 million and $46.8 million respectively. During this period Manley initiated an approach to Moscow but was disappointed to find that the Soviet Union was not interested in helping Jamaica with its economic difficulties. Knowledgeable sources subsequently indicated that the Soviets were skeptical of the ability of the PNP to administer socialist policies successfully and did not want to take on another economic burden in the Caribbean. Two years later Manley traveled to Moscow with equal lack of success.

The Jamaican economy still did not improve. In December 1977 Jamaica failed to meet the quarterly IMF test, and a new agreement for US$240 million over three years under the Extended Fund Facility was concluded in May 1978. It required further devaluation, reductions in budget expenditures, increased taxes, and limits on increases in wages. Manley bitterly describes this settlement as "one of the most savage packages ever imposed on any client government by the IMF."[17]

By 1979 the economic situation was approaching crisis proportions. Confidence in the PNP government had seriously eroded. Shortages of basic goods were common. Foreign exchange was scarce. Small shops were closing for lack of goods, as were factories for lack of raw materials or spare parts. The real estate market had collapsed. A modest increase in gasoline prices in April 1979 sparked spontaneous demonstrations in Kingston and elsewhere on the island, which the JLP quickly stimulated into a three-day general strike to protest continued PNP rule. Pressure on Manley to call an election before the end of his full five-year term in late 1981 was increasing. To reduce rising popular tensions, Manley announced in February 1980 that general elections would be held before the end of the year.

Dealing with the IMF became a critical ideological issue within the PNP after the 1977 agreement. In December 1979 Jamaica again failed an IMF test, and negotiations on a new agreement were soon under way. Facing the probability of cutting spending for popular social programs further and laying off thousands of government workers, the PNP resumed its internal debate over the IMF, which many in the party resented as an intrusive foreign authority. The debate centered on whether to follow a "dependent" economic model or to break with the IMF and seek an "alternative economic path" of self-reliance and help from friendly countries, such as OPEC members and socialist states. An economic commission within the PNP recommended that Jamaica break with the IMF, and in March 1980 the PNP national executive committee addressed the issue. It unanimously approved abandoning the IMF regimen in principle and voted, by a two-to-one margin, to do so immediately, rather than after the expiration of a new agreement, which would have allowed time to seek alternative sources of foreign exchange.

27

The decision meant that the government could avoid further adjustments desired by the IMF—a factor of considerable importance to a party facing a difficult reelection campaign. But it also meant denying the country essential foreign exchange. Efforts over the following months to obtain substitute sources of foreign exchange met with poor results, producing only small loans from Algeria and Iraq and several new lines of credit from European and Soviet bloc countries, including the Soviet Union. These were supplemented by advance borrowings from the aluminum companies on their quarterly levy payments and further delays in meeting foreign debt payments. But by mid-1980 Jamaica was bankrupt, desperately trying to get through the months until the election, after which it seemed probable that even a reelected PNP government would reach agreement with the IMF. Yet, surprisingly, the economy did not wholly collapse in 1980, an outcome avoided when the government began to approve "no-fund" import licenses to applicants controlling foreign exchange abroad, often obtained on the local black market from marijuana exporters, for whom business was thriving.

CONCLUSION

The Manley period lasted eight and a half years and, on balance, had disastrous results for Jamaica. In addition to the drastic economic deteriorioration of the country, many Jamaicans had lost confidence in their nation. Manley had held out great promise of necessary social change and economic improvement for poorer Jamaicans but had proved unable to achieve those goals without destabilizing the country. His programs proved to be extremely wasteful, and his consistent failure to adjust to the economic realities facing Jamaica only worsened the situation. Recent research in Kingston suggests that the income distribution gap widened during the 1970s as per capita income fell and much of the burden of the economic decline fell on the poor. The psychological destruction of Jamaican confidence in the 1970s, in a country where capital and labor are internationally mobile, may prove as damaging in the long run as the economic deterioration of the period. The loss of two generations of middle- and upper-class skilled Jamaicans (those who migrated and their children) has left a critical gap. The 1970s also saw rising crime, unprecedented political violence, and a flourishing narcotics traffic.

Although the record of the Michael Manley PNP administration is largely negative, it is clearly unfair to blame it for all Jamaica's problems during the decade. External economic factors were unfavorable, as were various internal characteristics of the island's society and economy, which together undermined PNP programs. Manley's successor is encountering similar obstacles to progress. The Manley record includes positive social initiatives, such as recognition of the rights of illegitimate children (in a society where 75 percent of births are illegitimate), an adult literacy program, and the dismantling of many race and class barriers. Perhaps the most lasting legacy of his regime is the increased sense of worth and participation many poorer Jamaicans gained during this period. Indeed, despite the economic disaster over which he presided, Manley remains highly popular with many of the country's poor. The PNP under Manley's leadership is still seen as the party most likely to pursue policies favoring the common man. In Jamaica's competitive political system, this is a powerful advantage and could well be a key to returning the PNP to power.

5

THE 1980 ELECTIONS: DEMOCRATIC CHANGE AMID POLITICAL VIOLENCE

The October 30, 1980, general election proved to be the most bitter, violent, and important in Jamaica's history. During the 1970s Jamaican politics had become increasingly polarized. The cordial and cooperative relations between Bustamante and Norman Manley were not repeated between Edward Seaga and Michael Manley, who have long shared a deep personal and ideological antagonism. This mutual distrust by the country's two principal political leaders filtered down through their two parties. Compounded with the widening ideological divergence between the Jamaica Labour Party and the People's National Party as the latter swung leftward, it caused rising political polarization between the rival camps and within the society as a whole.

Political rivalry was further intensified by a rampant spoils system known in Jamaica as political victimization, in which government-controlled jobs, housing, contracts, import licenses, and other benefits are given to supporters of the ruling party. With the economy in decline and the public sector a larger part of the total economy than ever before, victory at the polls in 1980 was seen as likely to lead to personal financial gains for supporters of the winning party.

By 1980 political polarization had come to have a class basis as well, one that could reflect a long-term change in Jamaican politics with important consequences. The centrist policies that both the JLP and the PNP followed before the Michael Manley administration reflected a system based on machine politics, which sought the support of as many groups as possible. Both parties usually had the backing of elements of the business and agricultural elites, the middle class, and the numerous urban and rural poor.

The PNP's shift to the left beginning in 1974 and its antibusiness and populist spending programs started a realignment from a reasonable balance of multiclass support in each party toward an increasingly class-based party system. This transformation was already evident in 1976 and reached its zenith in the 1980 elections. With the exception of die-hard adherents, the PNP lost most of its upper- and middle-class supporters. Some, including at least three PNP politicians who today are senior ministers in the government, switched to the JLP, while others took a neutral position. Even half the members of the PNP's union affiliate, the National Workers Union, voted for the JLP. The Seaga administration hopes to consolidate its power by retaining the multiclass support for the JLP. In contrast, the PNP, while paying lip service to the interests of the upper and middle classes, has yet to regain significant support among these groups. Should the PNP return to power committed to the pursuit of populist programs to the exclusion of the interests of other important groups, Jamaican politics could become more divisive, violent, and destabilized.

Violence and intense rumormongering further aggravated tension and mutual distrust during the 1980 campaign. Jamaicans are great palaverers, in an oral society where facts are often hard to obtain. In the climate of growing hate and fear in the 1970s, both sides were more and more willing to believe the worst of their opponents. Rumors significantly affected the political attitudes of the electorate. By 1980 the far left was beating the drums of destabilization and imminent coups ever louder, calling Seaga a bloodthirsty fascist and imperialist stooge. From Manley's opponents came charges that the country would become a Communist state if the PNP were returned to office and wild tales of Cuban intervention. Cuban submarines, it was said, had delivered arms at night. Cubans were allegedly training PNP guerrillas in the mountains above Kingston, fake Jamaican ballot boxes had been stuffed with pro-Communist votes in Havana, and small aircraft would infiltrate black Cuban troops into Jamaica on the eve of the election to disrupt voting in JLP areas. In the days immediately before the election, all flights out of the country were full, because of a rumor that the PNP would close the airports if victorious. None of these stories were true, but they were believed and repeated by many Jamaicans.

Jamaican politics has never been entirely free of violence, but before the mid-1960s such violence was limited to scuffles with fists, bottles, and stones. The illegal importation of revolvers and shotguns by criminals and the outbreak of gang warfare in Kingston slums eventually spilled over into increasingly violent clashes between supporters of the PNP and of the JLP. The contest in Seaga's West Kingston constituency in the months before the 1967 election between Seaga and Dudley Thompson—a leading PNP politician who was to hold the foreign affairs and national security portfolios in the 1970s—marked the first use of guns in Jamaican politics. Responsibility for this development is hard to assign, but in subsequent years politicians in both parties employed gunmen for political purposes. The 1972 and, especially, the 1976 and 1980 elections were marred by political killings.

In Jamaican politics violence is used to intimidate an opponent and his supporters as one means of influencing the final vote. But it also reflects the

31

passions of the lower classes, particularly in urban areas, who hope for patronage benefits when their party is in power. Both major political parties, as well as the Workers' Party of Jamaica, have employed and armed thugs and criminals at election time. In the crowded slums of Kingston, neighborhoods have been divided for many years along partisan lines, and armed gangs of criminals and unemployed youth with ties to political parties often clash. In 1980 many of the side streets of the capital were heavily barricaded to keep out rampaging gunmen from the other side.

At times in 1980 it seemed that the country's two "tribes"—the Socialists and the Labourites—were locked in a civil war. The elections were the bloodiest in the island's history; an estimated 600 persons died for political reasons, equivalent on a per capita basis to 60,000 in the United States.[18] The extreme violence that marred the 1980 elections was caused by the great political tension in the country, the unusual length of the campaign, which began soon after Manley's announcement in February that he would hold elections late in the year, the introduction of high-powered automatic rifles, and the inability of the overextended security forces to control the rising violence.[19]

The major issues for the Jamaican electorate in the elections were the state of the economy, a desire for a change in government, and a fear of Communism.[20] In contrast to the views of much of the foreign press reporting on the elections at the time, the elections were not seen in Jamaica as primarily an East-West contest between the United States and Cuba, although the results certainly had considerable effect on Jamaica's relations with those two countries.

Overwhelmingly, the Jamaican electorate was disturbed by the country's economic plight, for which it blamed the Manley government, and believed the JLP could turn the economy around and restore confidence. High unemployment, double-digit inflation, empty supermarket shelves, negative foreign investment, closed factories, poor administrative performance, wasteful government spending, corruption, and similar negative economic factors were widely seen as failures of the PNP regime. The PNP's defense of its accomplishments and its blaming external causes for the lack of greater success lost credibility among all but its hard-core supporters. The country was more impressed with JLP promises to bring about early economic improvement. Most of the electorate was convinced that the Manley government had done a poor job of running the country and that it was time again for a change of governing parties.

Fear of Communism was the second issue that worked heavily against the PNP in 1980. Most Jamaicans are Christian, anti-Communist, and highly individualistic. They became alarmed by the new closeness to Cuba, the radical rhetoric of the Manley government, and the influence Jamaican Communists were allowed in the publicly owned media and elsewhere.

The WPJ compounded the PNP's political problem by actively campaigning for PNP candidates. Seaga astutely played upon these popular fears by keeping the issue of Communism in full public view. The issue of violence also hurt the PNP, since many voters believed a JLP government would have more success in bringing crime and political violence under control.

The 1980 election is considered one of the fairest in Jamaica's political history, despite the high level of violence, which ceased almost entirely on the morning of election day. Electoral manipulation was sharply reduced, though not eliminated, by important reforms in electoral procedures adopted by Parliament in 1979 at the insistence of the opposition JLP, which threatened to boycott elections. These reforms established a bipartisan Electoral Commission composed of seven members, chaired independently of the government, with two representatives each from the JLP and the PNP, to oversee all aspects of the conduct of elections. The reforms also improved registration and voting procedures. The voters' list in 1980 was current, as it had not been in most previous elections, and an estimated 95 percent of eligible citizens registered. There was no last-minute gerrymandering as there had been by the JLP in 1972 and by the PNP in 1976. Incidents of multiple voting, ballot-box stuffing, theft of boxes and intimidation of voters and election officials by gunmen did occur, but they were less widespread than they would have been without the reforms and made no important difference to the final results.

Jamaican voters turned out in impressive numbers on October 30. Eighty-six percent of the registered voters went to the polls; an all-time high of 853,000 votes were cast. The JLP won an unprecedented 59 percent of the popular vote to a poor 41 percent for the PNP. Since Jamaica has a first-past-the-post rather than a proportional representation system, the winning party usually has a larger majority in the House of Representatives than in the popular vote. In 1980 the JLP was swept into office with fifty-one of the sixty seats, the most lopsided government-to-opposition ratio in Parliament in any of the country's elections.

The landslide JLP victory constituted both a strong rejection of the Manley period and a firm mandate to Seaga to improve the country's difficult situation. Despite the political turmoil that Jamaica went through in the late 1970s, the 1980 elections demonstrated that democracy can still function well in a troubled third world state. Manley proved his democratic credentials by calling the elections and by accepting the results, although the JLP and possibly the security forces would have caused him great difficulty if he had acted otherwise. The democratic tradition and the entrenched two-party system of the country permitted the Jamaican people to choose new leadership and an alternative approach to finding solutions to their serious problems.

Jamaica is more fortunate than most third world states, which lack institutionalized means of nonviolent political change. For this Caribbean nation, the democratic process and periodic alternation of the two parties in office have been forces for stability, although the political violence of recent years is a troublesome adjunct of the country's politics. The new ins usually have fresh approaches and are better motivated and less corrupt than the tired outs they replace. Popular enthusiasm after a change in government, at least for the first few years, is usually high.

Strong competition and alternation in power between the two parties constitute one of Jamaica's principal strengths. The party in power is acutely aware that it is likely to be voted out if it cannot perform well. But if its political history in the 1940s had been different, Jamaica would probably have developed into a one-party, socialist state with a stagnant economy and little hope of substantial economic progress, on the model of Guyana. Instead, Jamaica has had four peaceful changes of government during its forty years of democratic experience and, unlike all too many third world countries, has maintained its democratic tradition intact over more than two decades of independence. There is no guarantee that future strains and crises will not push Jamaican democracy toward authoritarian rule, but so far the country's political system has been able to absorb considerable stress and yet remain democratic.

6

THE SEAGA ADMINISTRATION:
JAMAICA STRUGGLES TO RECOVER

THE ECONOMY

The situation that Edward Seaga and his new Jamaica Labour Party administration inherited when he was sworn in on November 1, 1980, was grim.
The country was virtually bankrupt, with only enough foreign exchange for
two days' imports. Traditional agricultural exports were at their lowest in
decades. Manufacturing stood at 40 percent of capacity. Roads, schools,
hospitals, and other public services had badly deteriorated. Illiteracy was
rising; more than 50 percent of those leaving elementary school could
neither read nor write. The island's electrical generating system, a hodge-
podge of equipment from different countries, was improperly maintained
and often broke down. The political violence of the election campaign
would badly hurt the winter tourist season. Publicly owned enterprises
were losing massive amounts of money. The civil service was heavily over-
staffed and highly inefficient. Marijuana had become one of the island's
most valuable products while spreading corruption into many sectors of
society. The security forces were poorly equipped for their responsibilities,
and crime and violence remained major problems. Many of the guns used
for political purposes in 1980 soon filtered into the hands of criminals.
Unemployment and underemployment were very high. Essential profes-
sional and managerial skills were in short supply. Virtually every area of the
economy and the society was beset with problems.

In these circumstances the new government set economic recovery as
its principal objective. Seaga predicted it would take three years to achieve
substantial progress toward recovery and that during this period it would be
necessary to borrow heavily abroad to obtain sufficient foreign exchange to
stimulate new economic activity. By April 1981 he had concluded a three-
year Extended Fund Facility agreement with the IMF for US$698 million.
Large amounts of additional assistance were received in 1981 and subsequent years from other multilateral sources, private banks, and friendly
governments, led by the United States, whose assistance to Jamaica in-

creased several-fold. From 1981 to 1983 official U.S. assistance to Jamaica averaged about US$200 million annually, consisting each year of approximately US$50 million in balance-of-payments support, US$90 million in credits for U.S. foodstuffs, US$30 million in Agency for International Development projects, and US$40 million to purchase or barter for Jamaican bauxite for the U.S. strategic stockpile. Assistance will probably total the same US$200 million in 1984.

One of the hallmarks of the Seaga administration has been its aggressive campaign to attract investment from abroad. Seaga believes that Jamaica's future economic growth cannot be based primarily on further development of the bauxite and tourist industries and import substitution, as it was in the 1950s and 1960s. New engines of growth must be developed if there is to be significant economic development in the 1980s. He sees nontraditional agricultural and manufacturing exports as the two most promising possibilities and knows that foreign investment capital, technical expertise, and marketing connections are critical.

A new agency, Jamaica National Investment Promotion (JNIP), was established to match foreign investors' interest with potential new projects, while in the United States David Rockefeller, former Chase Manhattan Bank chairman, presided over a task force of prominent American businessmen to attract new investment to Jamaica. Similar groups were organized in Britain and Canada. But high interest rates and the severe recession in the United States and Europe meant that 1981 and 1982 were not good years in which to encourage interest in investing in countries like Jamaica, where numerous cultural, bureaucratic, and other impediments often frustrate potential investors. Militant trade unionism, a dilapidated infrastructure, high tax rates after the expiration of investment incentives, difficulties with remittances, foreign exchange shortages, and a bureaucratic nightmare of paper work and lethargic officialdom are among the internal factors that have discouraged investors and that the government has yet to remedy. More fundamentally, some investors who fear the return of People's National Party socialism do not assess the long-term investment climate in Jamaica as favorable.

Consequently, the flow of new investment to Jamaica has been less than had been optimistically predicted in 1981 and has yet to reach the pre-1973 amounts of more than US$100 million annually. By November 1983, 185 projects under JNIP auspices, with a capital investment of US$169 million, were in production. In addition, some capital returned to the country with the 20,000 to 30,000 Jamaicans who moved back to the island in 1981 and 1982, temporarily reducing net migration from Jamaica to its lowest in decades. In 1981 Jamaica lost only 5,900 more persons than it gained, down from 24,300 in 1980 and 9,800 in 1982. Although foreign investment has been less than anticipated, domestic investment began to pick up very substantially in early 1981 as local businesses expanded their operations and construction revived.

The JLP government has sought to put its domestic house in order as well as to attract overseas investment and borrowings. Efforts have been made to reduce the budget deficit each year, and further austerity measures have been taken in 1984. Tax collection has been intensified. The divestment of unprofitable public enterprises has proceeded slowly, but at the same time the government has unnecessarily acquired an oil refinery from Esso and stepped in to keep open several hotels that would otherwise have closed. Progress has been made in improving dilapidated public utilities and social services. Electricity failures have become less frequent because of improved maintenance and management of the power system, but a severe eighteen-month drought in 1982–1983 led to widespread water shortages in the capital area. Anxious that this problem not recur, the government will soon begin to install a new pipeline in the first major project in thirty years to ease Kingston's critical water situation.

Hospitals, schools, police stations, and other public buildings are slowly being repaired and better equipped. Partial compulsory education for children of primary school age is being introduced. A number of key highways and farm-to-market roads have also been improved. A great deal more needs to be done, and it seems likely that the quality of social and public services in Jamaica will remain badly handicapped by serious shortages of human and material resources for some time. Public sector employment will probably remain excessively high because of the political resistance to laying off workers unlikely to find other jobs.

A strong tourist sector has been one of the new government's economic successes, stimulated by its "Come back to Jamaica" advertising campaign. Arrivals reached an all-time high of 784,000 in 1983, a more than 25 percent increase over the preelection year of 1979. The island may soon be faced with undercapacity, and the construction of several new hotels is expected. Tourism will receive a new stimulus if a debate on permitting gambling in tourist areas results in government approval for hotel casinos.

Export growth has been disappointing for the past three years, reflecting chronic economic and bureaucratic problems and reduced demand created by the international recession. After a very slight increase in 1981, the value of exports fell by 10 percent in 1982 and stayed about the same in 1983. A sharp drop in bauxite and alumina shipments occasioned by the recession prevented what would otherwise have been a moderate improvement. Bauxite production, which stood at 12 million tons in 1980 and 11.6 million tons in 1981, plummeted to 8.6 million tons in 1982, the lowest level since 1968, and would have been as low as 7.0 million were it not for a US$32 million sale to the U.S. strategic stockpile. The revenue loss to the Jamaican government from reduced production levy and royalty payments from the bauxite-alumina companies was US$90 million in 1982. This was the most serious blow the new government has experienced in its efforts to obtain scarce foreign exchange and has forced further overseas borrowing and cutbacks in spending.

Even worse developments followed in 1983, when bauxite production fell to 7.3 million tons, the lowest in twenty years. Another U.S. purchase for its strategic stockpile and several counter-trade sales of bauxite together helped to avoid even more disastrous production levels. But with bauxite and alumina exports still constituting roughly 70 percent of the total value of Jamaica's exports, the slump in mining has had extremely adverse consequences for the balance of payments at a time when import demand has increased substantially because of the economic recovery program. Production of sugar and bananas has remained low because of chronic problems in those industries that the government has hardly begun to address. Exports of manufactured goods have also not grown significantly, largely because of insufficient supplies of raw materials. Although exports of agricultural and manufactured goods improved slightly in 1983, they did not compensate for the continuing depression in the bauxite-alumina sector. In late 1983 the government devalued the Jamaican dollar substantially and announced steps to simplify the cumbersome import-licensing system, which has seriously impeded manufacturing and exports.

Nineteen eighty-four is proving to be another disappointing year for the Jamaican economy. Foreign exchange will remain in short supply, and greater austerity is unavoidable. The closure of the Reynolds bauxite mine early in the year damaged hopes for a significant increase in bauxite and alumina production to 10.5 million tons as demand improved in the American and Canadian markets. Production is now expected to rise only to 8.5 million tons, or back to the depressed level of 1982. A brighter prospect, however, is for strong growth in the agricultural sector, reflecting the increased investment that is taking place, especially in nontraditional crops. Manufactured exports are also likely to rise. In early 1983 the government launched an ambitious new agricultural development program called Agro 21, which seeks to put much of the idle land in Jamaica to productive use, largely for export. Projects are now or will soon be operating under this program, which could eventually provide 38,000 new jobs, according to recent government statements. If successful, Agro 21 will be one of the principal accomplishments of the Seaga administration.

The economic picture in Jamaica thus remains extremely mixed, as long-term structural problems and negative external factors continue to dampen potential growth. Any overall assessment of the performance of the Jamaican economy in recent years, however, must give the JLP government credit for beginning to turn the economy around at a time of widespread contraction elsewhere in the hemisphere. Despite the unanticipated damage caused by the sharp drop in bauxite-alumina exports, there has been modest real growth for three successive years: 3.0 percent in 1981, 1.0 percent in 1982, and 1.1 percent in 1983. In late 1983 Jamaican government economists predicted 3 to 4 percent growth for 1984, but several months later other observers expected slightly negative growth. Inflation was held to single digits in 1981 (4.7 percent) and 1982 (6.7 percent) but rose to 18.5 percent in 1983 and reached 20 percent in the first six months of 1984 because of sharp increases in gasoline and electricity prices and a further devaluation of the Jamaican dollar. The unemployment rate fell slightly from 27.9 percent in April 1980 to 26.1 percent in April 1983, while the labor force increased by about 80,000, indicating that a significant number of new jobs are being created in the private sector.

Nevertheless, standards of living are not improving for the average Jamaican. Real per capita income has remained essentially the same for the last three years; average population growth is slightly above average real GDP growth. Although the seven-year slide in the Jamaican economy appears to have ended, it is likely to be some time before per capita income begins to rise. Furthermore, much stronger economic growth than can reasonably be expected would be needed to restore the standard of living that existed in Jamaica in the early 1970s.

In addition to being burdened by a dilapidated economy, highly mobile capital and skills, and weak confidence among the elite, Jamaica has a serious foreign debt problem from years of increasing borrowing. By 1983 per capita foreign debt exceeded US$1,000 and was approaching the per capita GDP income of US$1,300. These economic realities are likely to cause serious political problems for any Jamaican government, especially the JLP, which has based its appeal on promised economic performance.

Although the JLP government has been successful in stabilizing the economy and initiating a number of reformist economic policies, it has so far failed to establish an adequate basis for long-term progress. Much of the improvement in the past three years has come from sharply increased external assistance, intended to pump sufficient foreign exchange into Jamaica to revive the economy. Seaga deserves much credit for obtaining the loans and other forms of assistance that have helped him to stop the decline in economic growth. He has yet to find, however, the right formulas to stimulate the private sector sufficiently to lead to the increases in exports necessary to earn more foreign exchange. An overvalued exchange rate, ponderous licensing requirements and other bureaucratic impediments to manufacturing and export, and a plethora of inefficient and redundant state agencies have severely hampered export development. Under pressure from the IMF, the government, beginning in early 1983 and more drastically at the end of that year, sharply devalued the currency and greatly liberalized licensing arrangements for industries earning foreign exchange.[21] These actions should help recovery and export earnings, but Jamaica remains trapped in a statist economy in which the private sector and the free market are hampered by the inefficient workings of the public sector.

An interesting parallel exists between the difficulties of the present government with the IMF and those of its predecessor. The issues are remarkably similar: stimulating exports, diversifying agriculture, controlling inessential imports, reducing public sector employment and expenditures, and maintaining a realistic exchange rate. The structural problems of the economy have developed over many years and were exacerbated under Manley's rule, but they have changed relatively little in the almost seven years in which Jamaica has dealt with the IMF. Like his predecessor, Seaga has strongly resisted IMF conditions; but, unlike Manley, he has avoided an anti-IMF campaign that blames the IMF for Jamaica's economic problems. Seaga has spoken out for greater flexibility in the application of IMF conditions and for more financing to ease the current debt crisis, which so severely retards the economic progress of Jamaica and other developing countries.

FOREIGN POLICY

The Seaga administration has pursued a more traditional foreign policy than its predecessor. Foreign policy has been tied closely to economic recovery goals, in the words of Prime Minister Seaga, "to achieve a rational integration of foreign policy objectives and national interests."[22] The government's major foreign policy success has been to restore and maintain good relations with the United States. Seaga has formed close ties with President Ronald Reagan but without abandoning Jamaica's nonaligned position. Elected five days before the American president, Seaga was the first foreign leader to be received in the White House in 1981.

Renewed U.S. interest in Jamaica has helped the Jamaican recovery effort significantly. The U.S. administration in 1981 unrealistically viewed Jamaica as a model of how the free market and democracy could thrive in the third world. Jamaica has far to go to achieve self-sustained growth following free market or other policies. Stabilizing its economy and helping to preserve its democracy and its friendly relations with the United States require substantial U.S. help. U.S. bilateral assistance has reached high levels: Jamaica in 1981 and 1982 was the second highest per capita recipient of U.S. aid, after Israel. The purchase of Jamaican bauxite for the U.S. stockpile has helped reduce the foreign exchange loss from the slump in bauxite production. The resurgence of tourism and increased interest in the island by investors have been assisted by the more positive reputation Jamaica now has in the United States.

Jamaica has repaired its all-important relationship with the United States without reducing its sovereignty or becoming the U.S. lackey that its most vocal critics suggest. On key political and economic issues before the United Nations, for example, Jamaica generally votes with the position of the Non-Aligned movement, which almost always differs from that of the United States. In two areas in particular—South Africa and the Law of the Sea Treaty—Jamaica has strongly disagreed with U.S. policy. Nevertheless, convergence on certain international issues between Kingston and Washington is the basis of the perception of greater foreign policy agreement. These issues include Grenada, relations with Cuba, and support for the Caribbean Basin Initiative.

Jamaica's relations with Cuba have cooled a great deal under the JLP government. Ambassador Estrada was recalled by Havana at the request of the new government in early 1981, and diplomatic relations were, in effect, lowered to the chargé level at the desire of Kingston. Jamaican-Cuban relations could probably have continued on a normal basis had the Cubans not maintained their covert relationship with radical leftist elements in Jamaica. The issue came to a head in October 1981. Jamaica requested the return of three wanted criminals with ties to the PNP left whom it knew to be in Cuba. Havana denied any knowledge of their whereabouts, and Seaga angrily ordered the entire Cuban diplomatic staff in Kingston to depart. Cuba promptly removed its diplomats, as well as the two dozen Cuban medical personnel still working in Jamaica.

Seaga's action came after he was convinced that Cuba was continuing to interfere in Jamaica's internal affairs, despite the understanding he believed he had that Havana would end its relations with Jamaican subversive elements. The complete break in relations was a more severe act than seemed warranted; reducing the number of Cuban personnel to the size of the Jamaican embassy in Havana would have been less drastic. Seaga's move reflected his judgment of the seriousness of the Cuban offense and the decision of his government, with no encouragement from the U.S. Department of State, even though some have chosen to see the U.S. hand at work or suspect that Seaga's motive was to court Washington's favor. At no time did the United States seek to tie its support to Jamaica's diplomatic relations with Cuba.

The chilled state of relations with Cuba has not changed in three years since the break and is unlikely to improve soon in view of the profound belief of the present Jamaican government that promoting the political fortunes of the opposition parties remains Cuba's main interest in Jamaica. At the time of the rupture in diplomatic relations and on several subsequent occasions, the PNP has pledged to restore relations if it returns to office.

Elsewhere in the Caribbean Jamaica has pursued moderate policies.

41

Again, considerations of economic recovery have been foremost. Jamaica has sought and received assistance from Venezuela, Mexico, and even Puerto Rico, which the JLP government believes has much to teach its poorer English-speaking neighbors. In Central America the present Jamaican government differs sharply from the PNP in being concerned about the authoritarian political direction of Nicaragua and in supporting nonviolent solutions to the conflict in El Salvador, including the Contadora approach and the recommendations of the Kissinger Commission on Central America.

In the eastern Caribbean the JLP government has developed closer ties to the moderate leadership of Barbados and to the smaller Lesser Antilles governments, except Grenada. The Seaga administration viewed Prime Minister Maurice Bishop as the black sheep of the Caribbean Community (CARICOM) family and sought, unsuccessfully, to use CARICOM summit meetings in November 1982 and July 1983 to nudge Grenada toward elections and political liberalization. When Bishop was murdered in October 1983, Jamaica responded favorably to a request from the Organization of Eastern Caribbean States to send troops to Grenada to help replace the Coard-Austin military clique with a democratically elected government. Seaga has advocated strengthening the democratic, pro-Western, moderate regimes in the English-speaking Caribbean to reduce the possibility of future Grenadas. The arrest and murder of Bishop presented the Seaga government with one of its few foreign policy crises. Long concerned about Grenada's undemocratic practices and its close ties to Havana and Moscow, Seaga was deeply worried by the Coard-Austin takeover. He consulted extensively with eastern Caribbean leaders and eventually concluded with them that military action by a major power, the United States, was desirable. Like Barbados, Jamaica thus contributed to the invitation to the United States and did not respond, as some have charged, to a U.S. "master plan" to cloak its military action in Grenada with a regional cover.

Prime Minister Seaga has emerged as a spokesman for the Caribbean, seeking to bring the problems of Jamaica and the region to the attention of more affluent countries and international institutions. As early as 1980 he called for a major economic program to assist Caribbean states in the form of a "Caribbean Plan" with "special trade and investment preferences for the area." "A parade of warships in the Caribbean is not the solution," wrote Seaga at the time, for "if this better life escapes us, it is not only we who would have failed; the industrial democratic system would also have failed."[23] In 1981, as prime minister, Seaga expanded this idea into a call for a "Marshall Plan" for the region. He can thus take partial credit for inspiring the Caribbean Basin Initiative of the Reagan administration. On January 1, 1984, when the initiative became U.S. law, Jamaica and most other

42

countries in the region became beneficiaries of a twelve-year free trade access to the American market for most of their products.

DOMESTIC POLITICS

The political scene in Jamaica, which had been extremely quiet during 1981 and 1982 as the opposition found little reason to mount an early challenge, heated up quite unexpectedly in late 1983 when Seaga called early elections. The surprising response of the PNP in boycotting the elections has left the country in the unprecedented situation of having no opposition in Parliament. Thus 1984 has become a year of increased uncertainty for Jamaica, with its economy likely to decline slightly and its citizens uncomfortable over this new phase in the political contest between Seaga and Manley.

In calling elections for December 15, Seaga exercised his constitutional prerogative under the Westminster system to hold elections on short notice. Several factors appear to have influenced the decision to call an early poll rather than wait until the end of the JLP's full five-year term in late 1985. First and most important, the JLP was confident of winning early elections but could not be as certain of victory at a later date. Like any other party in a democratic system, its goal is to remain in office, and the tactic of a snap election is a legitimate means for this purpose.

Second, the tighter foreign exchange situation of mid-1983 led to Jamaica's failing its September IMF test, although the government's position is that the two parties disagreed over calculations and there was no actual failure. Both the Jamaican government and the IMF subsequently agreed in principle to substitute a new fifteen-month standby loan of US$180 million for the remaining US$80 million that Jamaica could draw upon under the 1981 Extended Fund Facility agreement. As a precondition to the new agreement, Jamaica agreed to a full devaluation of the Jamaican dollar in place of the partial devaluation of January 1983. Other austerity measures required by the new agreement were the focus of difficult negotiations in the first months of 1984. These measures are certain to cause the government political problems when their full effect is felt. No doubt the anticipated effect of the IMF conditions helped determine the timing of the elections.

Third, the popularity of the JLP government temporarily increased after Jamaica participated in the joint military action in Grenada in late October, which Jamaicans favored by a 56 percent majority, according to a Stone poll. In a related development, several statements by Manley in early November criticizing the intervention and declaring his intention to restore ties with Cuba, as well as an intemperate attack in Parliament by Seaga on

43

PNP officials who have traveled to Havana and Moscow, drew renewed attention to the issue of PNP ties to Communist countries. The periodic opinion polls of Stone have been a good indicator of the popularity of the two parties. His polls showed the JLP ahead for its first two years in office and the opposition ahead of the government since October 1982, except for a brief period at the time of the events in Grenada when the JLP temporarily regained its lead.[24]

Fourth, the opposition did not expect elections, despite hints by Seaga, and had few candidates in place and inadequate financial resources for a campaign. Nevertheless, fearful of a snap election, the PNP had warned the government as early as May that it would not contest elections until a new voters' list was ready.

Seaga did not have the immediate support of his party to seek a new mandate. Some were not prepared for an early campaign. Others felt the JLP could win an election in the spring when new lists based on a 1983 voter registration drive would be ready, thereby avoiding a likely opposition criticism of foul play. When Seaga first approached his senior party colleagues in mid-November, he did not obtain the consensus on snap elections that he wanted. Rumors of an early election soon spread in Kingston, and a week later the party was united behind Seaga's position. The immediate cause of the change was a vitriolic statement by PNP General Secretary Paul Robertson on November 24, which attacked Seaga for not giving the country details of the IMF negotiations, termed his behavior "immoral, cowardly, and dictatorial," and called for his resignation as finance minister. Seaga responded quickly, announcing the next day, after winning the support of his senior lieutenants, that he had asked the governor general for early elections. Had it not been for Robertson's attack, Seaga might have waited for the new voters' list to hold local and general elections close to each other in February or March 1984.

Manley and PNP Chairman P. J. Patterson were abroad when Robertson issued his intemperate statement and rushed home for an emergency party meeting after the election announcement. Some within the PNP favored contesting the elections. They were certain the PNP could increase its representation in Parliament and believed the opposition had the responsibility to give the electorate a choice. Manley, however, argued for a boycott. This already was his stated public position, and he knew the party was not sufficiently prepared to win. A boycott was also likely to create a political controversy, which, along with the expected economic hardships, might swing public opinion increasingly against the government and force early elections in 1985 or 1986. Publicly the PNP charged that the elections were "bogus" because the JLP had broken what the PNP considered an obligation to hold elections on the new list.[25] The PNP pointed out that the new list would add some 100,000 voters who had reached eighteen between 1980 and 1983, a group likely to favor the opposition.

With the PNP out of the race, fifty-four of the sixty JLP candidates ran unopposed. The remaining six had no trouble defeating their obscure opponents in the polls on December 15. To no one's surprise, turnout was extremely low.

The outcome of the 1983 elections was unprecedented in Jamaica's political history. Although the JLP boycotted relatively unimportant local elections in 1977 on the grounds that major electoral reforms needed to be put in place first, neither party had ever refused to contest general elections. And no Jamaican Parliament has ever been without some official opposition representation. The new Parliament sworn in January 10 has a House of Representatives in which all sixty seats are occupied by the JLP, and the eight nongovernment members of the Senate are non-PNP independents nominated by the prime minister. The constitutional position of leader of the opposition, by law filled by the leader of the largest nongovernment group in the House, is vacant for the first time.

Had the PNP fought the elections, it is likely that its representation in Parliament would have increased to between fifteen and twenty-five of the sixty seats, according to well-informed Jamaican observers. This result would have avoided the present odd political situation. Instead, both Seaga and Manley have strained the rules that tie the fabric of Jamaican democracy together. Both parties had agreed in 1979 to the electoral reforms favored by the JLP, then in opposition. The reforms were honored in 1980, when an updated voters' list was prepared under considerable time pressure. Even though a new voters' list was only a few months from completion in late 1983, Seaga decided to use the 1980 list. Manley was not prepared to contest a snap election and, like Seaga, chose a course that weakened the norms of democratic political competition in Jamaica.

Most Jamaicans do not like a one-party Parliament, are critical of both Seaga and Manley for bending the rules, and favor early elections to resolve the issue. In a December 1983 Stone poll, Jamaicans by a 70 to 26 percent margin favored new elections when the voters' list is ready and by a 59 to 38 percent majority disapproved holding elections on the old list. Although the government is legal, not bogus as the opposition charges, its status has suddenly become a controversial domestic political issue. The JLP holds the view, not surprisingly, that the government has behaved constitutionally and that the opposition abdicated its proper role by its boycott. With a new five-year term lasting until early 1989, Seaga is unlikely to call elections until he is fairly confident of winning. That will depend to a great extent on achieving the economic recovery that still eludes his country. An early electoral test may occur in local government elections, which in April 1984 the Parliament voted to delay for one year, until June 1985, on the grounds that the voters' list was still incomplete.

The new political situation will require restraint by both sides if a serious political crisis is to be avoided. The JLP should not make the mistake of believing that the one-party Parliament reflects its true popularity and must be careful to avoid actual or apparent abuses of power. "Crawling peg dictatorship" is a fear already expressed by one of Jamaica's leading commentators. The government has introduced a procedure allowing members of the public to make presentations to the House in the absence of anyone to speak officially for the opposition, but few have used this arrangement. Moreover, the eight non-JLP senators are respected persons who are proving to be articulate critics of the government.

The PNP may have a difficult job of presenting itself as the alternative government without a parliamentary platform and will have to find new ways to keep its views before the public. Manley has named "constituency representatives" in each of the sixty districts to discuss key issues with voters and is holding periodic meetings of a "People's Forum" to discuss matters of public interest. The PNP is also working to rebuild its political machinery, acquire a more moderate image, and surmount the bitter personality and ideological quarrels of past years. In the first large political demonstration in Jamaica since the 1980 elections, thousands of PNP supporters marched peacefully in Kingston on January 10, 1984, to protest the opening of the "bogus" Parliament.

As the hardships caused by continuing economic austerity spread, the contest for power between the two parties may grow heated and be reflected in increased demonstrations, trade union turbulence, and political violence. Jamaica is entering a period of painful economic adjustment with its political situation more polarized than at any time since the 1980 elections. Whether the country can focus its energies on essential economic priorities or will be diverted into a potentially destructive political struggle will affect economic recovery and, perhaps, the future of the nation's parliamentary democracy. At midyear the two-party system remained vibrant; discussion of issues in the Senate, in the PNP forum, and in the media permitted frequent criticism of the government; and violent confrontation did not seem imminent.

7

CONCLUSIONS

In 1984 Jamaica remains a lower-middle-income, democratic, developing state, which has suffered severe economic and political deterioration for a decade. The inability of its economy to adjust to the oil price shocks of the 1970s, the inappropriate domestic and foreign policies of the Manley government, the effects of the 1981–1982 recession on its vulnerable economy, and continuing structural impediments to growth have left it economically weak. Many of its problems are chronic ones for which there are no quick or easy solutions. Jamaica will continue to require substantial foreign assistance and investment for some time if it is to avoid further social disruption and political instability. Internally, however, several key areas that the country is capable of improving would help it to survive the difficult period ahead.

A. Jamaica needs to find a way to restore consensus politics. Polarization in the society is too extreme. It leads to sharp swings in policy, violence, victimization, preoccupation with politics rather than national development, excessive distrust among leaders, an unattractive investment climate, exaggerated trade union rivalry, and other inefficiencies. Maintaining multiclass parties and elite consensus on the rules governing political competition is critical to stability. Achieving national agreement on an agenda of priorities would help the country focus on solutions to its major problems while permitting political debate over means of implementation without the poisoned extremism of recent years. Unfortunately, there are few signs of any emerging policy consensus. Although politics was greatly subdued in 1981 and 1982, the two parties and their leaders have remained highly antagonistic and distrustful of each other. Some initial efforts at cooperation in mid-1983, such as talks between the two general secretaries to devise means of controlling future political violence and the formation of a bipartisan group to deal with the growing narcotics problem, were suspended by the snap elections. Consensus building has a low priority, and confrontation politics remains the norm.

B. The engine of economic growth for the 1980s should be the development of agriculture and light manufacturing for export. Improvement of the tourist and mining sectors is important but insufficient to bring about substantial economic growth. The economy depends excessively on overseas borrowing and narcotics to obtain needed foreign exchange. There are already signs of slow improvement in agriculture and manufacturing. The Caribbean Basin Initiative free trade zone should help increase exports of traditional Jamaican products, such as rum and cigars, as well as stimulate foreign and local investment in the manufacture of new products on the island. There is a good chance of significant increases in foreign investment and export growth over the next several years as long as the political climate is propitious.

C. Jamaicans need to regain confidence in their country and to become better able to place national discipline and sacrifice above personal gratification. A continuation of capital flight, which rose sharply in late 1983, and the migration of needed skills have a crippling effect on prospects for substantial growth. Jamaican elites have not yet developed a commitment to social transformation. These weaknesses of national discipline and patriotism also fragment the society and make it difficult to achieve consensus and agreement on a national agenda. Unfortunately, there are few signs that this situation is changing.

D. The maintenance of good relations between the United States and Jamaica should have the highest priority among the foreign policy objectives of any Jamaican government because of the great importance of the United States to the Jamaican economy—in trade, tourism, investment, mining, and other areas. Self-reliance for a small state such as Jamaica in an interdependent world is a formula for isolation and economic disaster. Nevertheless, there remains a strongly anti-American political element in Jamaica that, though not influential now, might cause the country serious problems if the political situation should again shift to the left. For the present, both the government and the opposition recognize the importance of relations with the United States, although some fear that if the People's National Party should return to power, it might again pursue policies that would harm bilateral relations. Such a possibility cannot be dismissed and underscores the importance of a continuing dialogue between the United States and all responsible leaders in Jamaica.

NOTES TO TEXT

This study, based primarily on the author's direct experience in Jamaica, is a synthesis of information acquired in countless discussions with Jamaicans and in the reading of local documents and background material, supplemented by specific research. The author is indebted to all who have advised and supported him in this project, especially his many friends and interlocutors in Jamaica, the faculty, staff, and fellows of the Center for International Affairs at Harvard University, and his colleagues in the State Department and the Agency for International Development.

1. As many persons of Jamaican origin are believed to live in other countries as in Jamaica. Sizable Jamaican communities exist in the United States, Canada, the United Kingdom, Panama, Cuba, Costa Rica, and Nicaragua. Jamaica has the highest per capita rate of emigration to the United States of any country. The propensity of many Jamaicans to seek better lives elsewhere is unlikely to change in the foreseeable future.

2. For an up-to-date description of human rights observance in Jamaica, see the annual State Department human rights report, published in U.S. Department of State, *Country Reports on Human Rights Practices for 1983* (Washington, D.C., 1984), pp. 616–23.

3. John Charles Gannon, "The Origins and Development of Jamaica's Two-Party System, 1930–1975" (Ph.D. dissertation, Washington University, St. Louis, Missouri, 1976), p. 97.

4. Ibid., p. 158.

5. Five leaders, three of them with trade union backgrounds, have dominated Jamaican politics since the 1930s. William Alexander Bustamante and Norman Manley were unrivaled during the first two and a half decades of self-rule and independence; Michael Manley, Hugh Shearer, and Edward Seaga have been the principal political figures since 1970. The following list of Jamaica's political leaders illustrates the alternation in office of the JLP and the PNP every two elections since 1944.

Year of Election	*Winning Party*	*Chief Minister, Premier, Prime Minister*
1944	JLP	Alexander Bustamante
1949	JLP	Alexander Bustamante
1955	PNP	Norman Manley
1959	PNP	Norman Manley
1962	JLP	Alexander Bustamante
1967	JLP	Donald Sangster
		Hugh Shearer (succeeded Sangster, who died seven weeks after the election)
1972	PNP	Michael Manley

Year of Election	Winning Party	Chief Minister, Premier, Prime Minister
1976	PNP	Michael Manley
1980	JLP	Edward Seaga
1983	JLP	Edward Seaga

6. Figures are drawn from Owen Jefferson, *The Post-War Economic Development of Jamaica* (Kingston: Institute of Social and Economic Research, University of the West Indies, 1972).

7. Shearer is the most significant labor figure in Jamaica today. Although he was named deputy prime minister and minister of foreign affairs in the Seaga administration in 1980, he has retained the presidency of the BITU and actively runs the union from behind the scenes.

8. Like Norman Manley and Bustamante, Michael Manley and Shearer are distant cousins. This has helped them to maintain friendly communications despite their political differences.

9. People's National Party, "Principles and Objectives," Kingston, February 1979, pp. 52–53.

10. The government has considerable control over the broadcast media in Jamaica. The island's single television station is government owned, as is one of the two radio stations. The press is dominated by the century-old privately owned *Daily Gleaner,* which has had no rival since a government-owned newspaper failed in 1983. Radical journalists were influential to an unprecedented extent from 1974 to 1981, producing a slant on the news that most Jamaicans disliked.

11. The author had occasion to witness Estrada's behavior when seated behind him and a Cuban Communist delegation at the October 5, 1980, public session of the PNP annual conference. When Manley, at the end of a lengthy political address, announced the date of the elections, Estrada, who had been sipping rum for several hours, rose to join in the general celebration by the large crowd of PNP supporters. He made a special point of shouting into the author's ear one phrase from the PNP campaign song of that year, to which the crowd and he were gyrating. The words—"Down with imperialism; socialism forever!"—summarized the ambassador's view of his mission in Jamaica.

12. Michael Manley, *Jamaica: Struggle in the Periphery* (London: Third World Media, 1982).

13. Ibid., pp. 216, 219.

14. Many of these charges are conveniently assembled in an appendix entitled "Destabilization Diary" in ibid., pp. 223–37.

15. Ibid., p. 199.

16. Judicial review of election results can be a lengthy process. All but one of these challenges were eventually dropped, and in the one case completed the seat was awarded to the JLP.

17. Manley, *Jamaica,* p. 160.

18. The vast majority of these killings have never been solved by the hard-pressed government authorities, and there have been no convictions in the few cases of political murder that have been tried. The number 600 was arrived at by subtracting the average number of murders for the two years before the election

year from the total number in 1980. Once the elections were over, violence abated. The number of murders fell to 521 in 1981 and to 447 in 1982.

19. In addition to the hundreds of M-16s from Cuba, weapons reached Jamaica illegally from other sources. The country's airspace and coastline are virtually undefended, so that the smuggling of contraband is fairly easy. Small planes and boats that come to the island to pick up marijuana can easily bring in weapons. It is very difficult for U.S. enforcement agencies to stop unlicensed exports of small arms from leaving the United States in this fashion.

20. Jamaica's leading public opinion analyst, Carl Stone, obtained the following results in a February 1981 poll:

Question: Why do you think so many voters voted for the JLP across the country?

Answers:	(% giving reason)
1. Economic hardships	31
2. Fear of Communism	26
3. Time for a change of government	19
4. Voters fed up with PNP mismanagement	16
5. Greater appeal of Seaga as someone likely to run the country better than Manley	13

Carl Stone, *The Political Opinions of the Jamaican People (1976–81)* (Kingston: Blackett Publishers, 1982), p. 12.

21. By mid-1984 the Jamaican dollar had fallen to less than US$0.25 from US$0.56 in 1981 and was expected to decline further.

22. Edward Seaga, ''Report to the Parliament on the Administration's Third Year in Office,'' November 29, 1983, Jamaica Information Service, Kingston, p. 3.

23. Edward Seaga, ''The Jamaica Labour Party Foreign Policy Guidelines,'' Kingston, 1980, p. 7.

24. *Date of Poll*	*JLP*	*PNP*	*WPJ*	*Uncommitted*
			(percent)	
October 1980	50	37	—	13
February 1981	46	29	—	25
May 1981	48	20	—	30
July 1981	36	32	—	31
November 1981	36	30	2.0	31
May 1982	41	34	0.6	24
October 1982	38	43	0.3	19
March 1983	38	41	1.0	20
October 1983	43	38	0.5	19
December 1983	32	39	0.3	29

25. Jamaica's cumbersome but fair registration procedures have meant that many elections have been held on voter lists that have not been up to date. This was not the case, however, in 1976 and 1980. In 1976 a new list had been prepared to reflect the lowering of the voting age from twenty-one to eighteen. In 1980 the PNP honored an agreement with the JLP to wait until a new list was ready before

holding elections, one of the factors that made that year's campaign so long. Snap elections are unusual in Jamaica. The only precedent is 1962, when Norman Manley called a general election three years into his second term, after losing the referendum that led to Jamaican withdrawal from the West Indies Federation.

BIBLIOGRAPHY

For readers who wish to investigate Jamaica in more detail, a list of books on the country's history, politics, and economy follows. Unfortunately, no recent work provides a general, comprehensive account of political and economic developments in postindependence Jamaica. Several of those listed below, however, are valuable reference sources on aspects of contemporary Jamaica.

Black, Clinton V. *The Story of Jamaica: From Prehistory to the Present*. London: Collins, 1965.

Brown, Aggrey. *Color, Class, and Politics in Jamaica*. New Brunswick, N.J.: Transaction Books, 1980.

Eaton, George E. *Alexander Bustamante and Modern Jamaica*. Kingston: Kingston Publishers, 1975.

Hamilton, B. L. St. John. *Problems of Administration in an Emergent Nation: A Case Study of Jamaica*. New York: Praeger, 1964.

Jefferson, Owen. *The Post-War Economic Development of Jamaica*. Kingston: Institute of Social and Economic Research, University of the West Indies, 1972.

Kaplan, Irving, et al. *Area Handbook for Jamaica*. Washington, D.C.: Government Printing Office, 1976.

Knight, Franklin W. *The Caribbean: The Genesis of a Fragmented Nationalism*. New York: Oxford University Press, 1978.

Lacey, Terry. *Violence and Politics in Jamaica, 1960–1970: Internal Security in a Developing Country*. London: F. Cass, 1977.

Lewis, Gordon K. *The Growth of the Modern West Indies*. New York: Monthly Review Press, 1968.

Lowenthal, David. *West Indian Societies*. New York: Oxford University Press, 1972.

Manley, Michael. *Jamaica: Struggle in the Periphery*. London: Third World Media, 1982.

———. *The Politics of Change: A Jamaican Testament*. Washington, D.C.: Howard University Press, 1975.

———. *A Voice at the Workplace*. London: Andre Deutsch, 1975.

Nettleford, Rex. *Caribbean Cultural Identity: The Case of Jamaica*. Los Angeles: UCLA Latin American Center Publications, 1978.

Nettleford, Rex, ed. *Manley and the New Jamaica: Speeches and Writings, 1938–1968*. London: Longman Caribbean, 1971.

Palmer, Ransford W. *The Jamaican Economy*. New York: Praeger, 1968.

Parry, J. H., and P. M. Sherlock. *A Short History of the West Indies*. London: Macmillan, 1956.

Sherlock, Philip. *Norman Manley: A Biography*. London: Macmillan, 1980.

Stone, Carl. *Class, Race, and Political Behaviour in Urban Jamaica*. Kingston: Institute of Social and Economic Research, University of the West Indies, 1973.

———. *Democracy and Clientelism in Jamaica*. New Brunswick, N.J.: Transaction Books, 1980.

———. *Electoral Behaviour and Public Opinion in Jamaica*. Kingston: Institute of Social and Economic Research, University of the West Indies, 1974.

———. *The Political Opinions of the Jamaican People (1976–81)*. Kingston: Blackett Publishers, 1982.

Stone, Carl, and Aggrey Brown. *Perspectives on Jamaica in the 1970s*. Kingston: Jamaica Publishing House, 1980.

Stone, Carl, and Aggrey Brown, eds. *Essays on Power and Change in Jamaica*. Kingston: Department of Government, University of the West Indies, 1976.

Selected AEI Publications

AEI Foreign Policy and Defense Review (four issues $18; single copy $5.00)

In Search of Policy: The United States and Latin America, Howard J. Wiarda (1984, 147 pp., cloth $17.95, paper $7.95)

Rift and Revolution: The Central American Imbroglio, Howard J. Wiarda, ed. (1984, 392 pp., cloth $19.95, paper $10.95)

Small Countries, Large Issues, Mark Falcoff (1984, 126 pp., cloth $14.95, paper $5.95)

The Crisis in Latin America: Strategic, Economic, and Political Dimensions, Howard J. Wiarda, ed., with Mark Falcoff and Joseph Grunwald (1984, 32 pp., $2.95)

Interaction: Foreign Policy and Public Policy, Don C. Piper and Ronald J. Terchek, eds. (1983, 235 pp., cloth $16.95, paper $8.95)

The Reagan Phenomenon—and Other Speeches on Foreign Policy, Jeane J. Kirkpatrick (1983, 230 pp., $14.95)

U.S. Interests and Policies in the Caribbean and Central America, Jorge I. Dominguez (1982, 55 pp., $4.75)

• *Mail orders for publications to:* AMERICAN ENTERPRISE INSTITUTE, 1150 Seventeenth Street, N.W., Washington, D.C. 20036 • *For postage and handling, add 10 percent of total; minimum charge $2, maximum $10 (no charge on prepaid orders)* • *For information on orders, or to expedite service, call toll free 800-424-2873 (in Washington, D.C., 202-862-5869)* • *Prices subject to change without notice.* • *Payable in U.S. currency through U.S. banks only*

AEI Associates Program

The American Enterprise Institute invites your participation in the competition of ideas through its AEI Associates Program. This program has two objectives: (1) to extend public familiarity with contemporary issues; and (2) to increase research on these issues and disseminate the results to policy makers, the academic community, journalists, and others who help shape public policies. The areas studied by AEI include Economic Policy, Education Policy, Energy Policy, Fiscal Policy, Government Regulation, Health Policy, International Programs, Legal Policy, National Defense Studies, Political and Social Processes, and Religion, Philosophy, and Public Policy. For the $49 annual fee, Associates receive

- a subscription to *Memorandum,* the newsletter on all AEI activities
- the AEI publications catalog and all supplements
- a 30 percent discount on all AEI books
- a 40 percent discount for certain seminars on key issues
- subscriptions to any two of the following publications: *Public Opinion,* a bimonthly magazine exploring trends and implications of public opinion on social and public policy questions; *Regulation,* a bimonthly journal examining all aspects of government regulation of society; and *AEI Economist,* a monthly newsletter analyzing current economic issues and evaluating future trends (or for all three publications, send an additional $12).

Call 202/862-6446 or write: AMERICAN ENTERPRISE INSTITUTE
1150 Seventeenth Street, N.W., Suite 301, Washington, D.C. 20036

DATE DUE

DEMCO 38-297